PRAISE FOR

Dr. David R. Pearce
& Peak Success

As you read David's book, you will be exposed to new ways of thinking about your practice goals and systems. He uses his own life experiences to demonstrate what is possible when we design our practice with an endpoint in mind. Using specific systems and proven methodologies, he outlines how a dentist can learn to "think well" by recognizing, and then altering, thinking patterns that prevent them from reaching their goals and achieving the prosperity they desire. This book provides strong management support to dentists by offering a step-by-step program to improve a dentist's leadership capacity. David carefully explains and presents the systems necessary to carry that leadership into improved office systems, team performance, and patient treatment acceptance. This is a comprehensive guide to defining your vision, creating an action plan, and achieving your goals.

—DR. JOHN KOIS
FOUNDER AND CEO, KOIS CENTER, SEATTLE, WA

In more than two decades of professional consulting for business owners of all walks of life, I have never met a man more capable of turning business owners into wealth entrepreneurs more so than Dr. David Pearce. You are about to embark on a journey of prosperity creation, business mastery and most importantly personal potential discovery. In Dr. Pearce's new book, he takes the *War of Art* and *Good to Great* and shakes them up into a battle plan for success that will give you a rock solid business, a powerful life of fulfillment and an unlimited abundance of wealth in every way. His ability to get to the heart of the matter while being relatable and funny will help you gain clarity, confidence, and the ability to make more profitable decisions. Prepare yourself for a hard hitting, and heartfelt, book that will challenge your thinking, expand your horizons, open your eyes, and have you breaking through every single thing that is holding you back in life, business, and prosperity.

—SCOTT J. MANNING, MBA
WWW.MILLIONDOLLARMETHODS.COM
WWW.DENTALSUCCESSTODAY.COM

Dr. Pearce has done a wonderful job of identifying, simplifying, and providing a step-by-step process to one of the greatest barriers that we see in advanced dentistry today: getting patients to say yes to the amazing dental treatment we offer. Many dentists become clinical masters, but they can't successfully create an office where staff change patients from someone who doesn't believe dentistry can help them to someone who gratefully writes a large check to remove their dental disabilities. This book provides the framework needed to push your business to levels that elude many highly trained dentists for their entire careers. Dr. Pearce also provides a logical and much needed roadmap to manage business revenue and to assure the owner's financial success and wealth accumulation. This book is a must read for any dentist (or small business entrepreneur) who wants to overcome the frustration of knowing they can do more, help patients say yes to life changing dentistry, and predictably accumulate wealth that provides real financial freedom.

—RANDOLPH R. RESNIK, DMD
DIRECTOR AND FOUNDER OF RESNIK
IMPLANT INSTITUTE

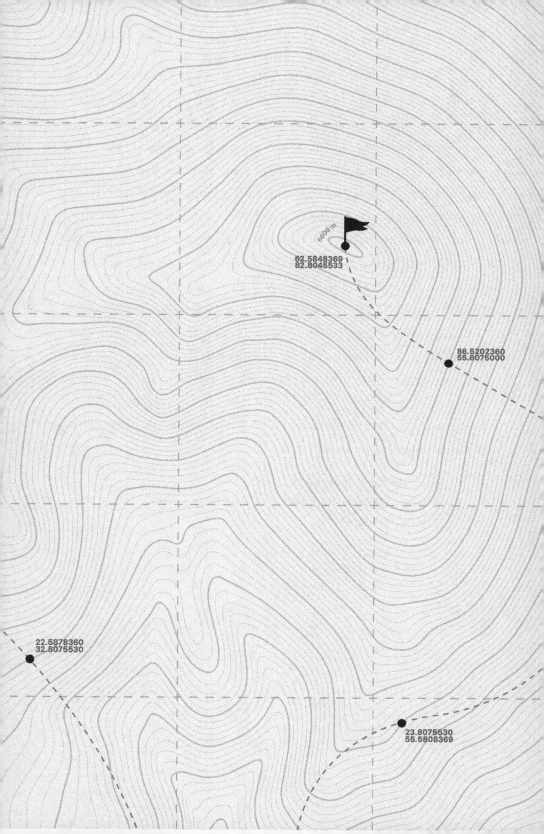

PEAK
SUCCESS

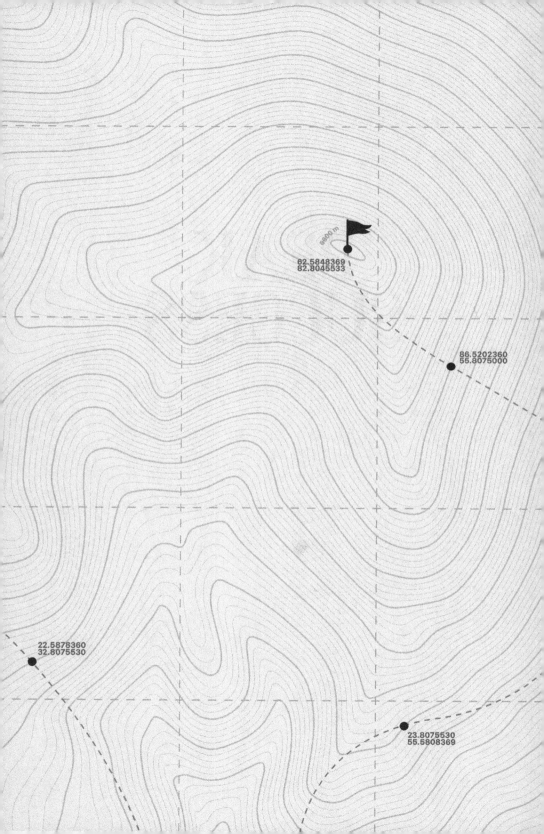

DR. DAVID R. PEARCE

PEAK SUCCESS

AN ENTREPRENEURIAL GUIDE TO BUSINESS PROSPERITY

Advantage | Books

Published by Advantage Books, Charleston, South Carolina.
An imprint of Advantage Media.

ADVANTAGE is a registered trademark, and the Advantage colophon is a trademark of Advantage Media Group, Inc.

Printed in the United States of America.

10 9 8 7 6 5 4 3 2 1

ISBN: 978-1-64225-877-6 (Paperback)
ISBN: 978-1-64225-876-9 (eBook)

Library of Congress Control Number: 2023913927

Cover and layout design by David Taylor.

This publication is designed to provide accurate and authoritative information in regard to the subject matter covered. It is sold with the understanding that the publisher is not engaged in rendering legal, accounting, or other professional services. If legal advice or other expert assistance is required, the services of a competent professional person should be sought.

Advantage Books is an imprint of Advantage Media Group. Advantage Media helps busy entrepreneurs, CEOs, and leaders write and publish a book to grow their business and become the authority in their field. Advantage authors comprise an exclusive community of industry professionals, idea-makers, and thought leaders. For more information go to **advantagemedia.com**.

Behind every great man, there stands a great woman.

While this statement is merely an observation by many, it rings true as they observe the small and large feats of man over the ages. For me, my wife, Susan, has been the behind-the-scenes support that allowed me to devote the time to create this book and gave me the encouraging push to believe I am capable of producing a sought-after manuscript.

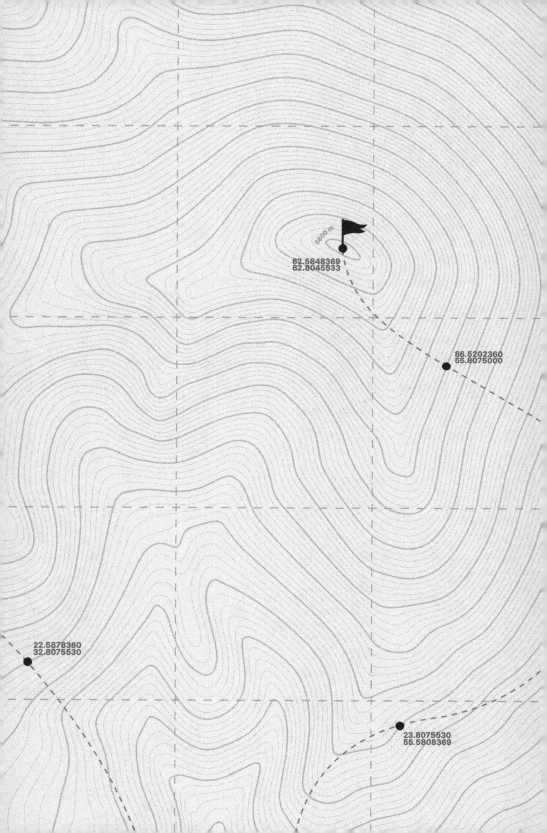

Contents

PART IV
BUILDING WEALTH

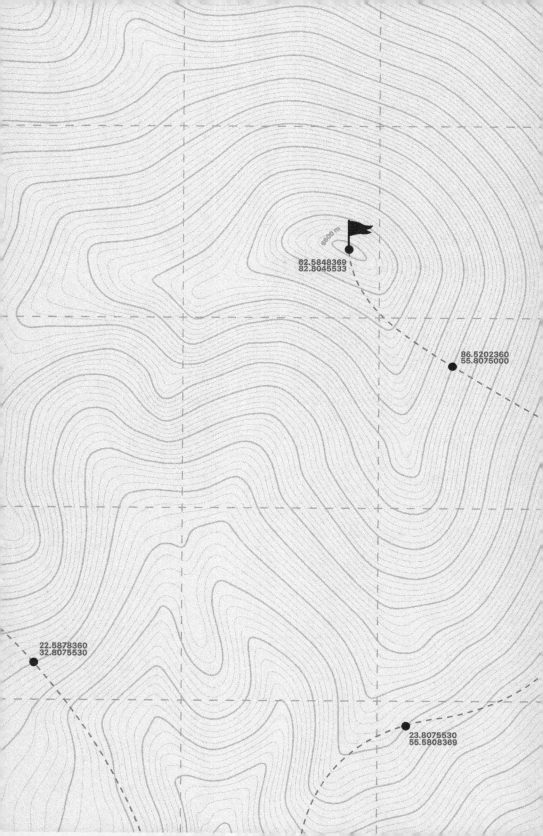

Introduction

My wife and I share a giggle when we travel. She is about the destination, and I am about the journey. We are both right, though our focus is different. It would be foolish to think Susan isn't thinking about how she gets from the beginning to the end. She is a trained opera singer, and I watch her painstakingly dissect an operatic piece by repeatedly singing a few measures until they are just right, then moving on to the next measures. Yet she says she does it all for the show itself, crossing the "finish line" and hearing the applause of the patrons as the singers take their final bow at the last curtain. For me, it's embracing the process and the work required to create the end result. To a fault, I don't focus or acknowledge the victory like I do the required actions and work needed to reach the next level of success.

Dental-practice ownership is a journey. Early in my dental career, I was a poor leader. I expected poor conversations with my team, and I predicted that patients wouldn't accept my treatment recommendations. As my thinking improved and my leadership skills grew, my practice rose to the top 1 percent. My team of six worked four days per week, closed the office for twelve to fourteen weeks per year, collected $18,000 to $20,000 per day, and pushed revenue toward $3 million. Our personal net worth soared past $10 million. I traveled around the world to pursue my hobby of high-altitude backpack hunting and built my wife's dream contemporary beach house and our Montana mountain retreat. I didn't start off with any of those aspirations. I only wanted to become the best I could be.

Perhaps the greatest acknowledgments of my personal and professional growth were the positive testimonials from countless patients who made huge investments in themselves to change their lives through dental reconstruction. I was also honored to receive many wonderful letters from team members telling me they had become better versions of themselves while working with me and how much they appreciated me and our time together.

At age thirty-five, I had an aching feeling that I would not be able to create significant good in the world because I wouldn't have enough talent or wealth to make a huge impact. A wise friend said to me, "Do unto one what you wish you could do for the world." That thought "seed" got planted and germinated in my soul. Our office mantra, "Changing people's lives, one smile at a time," aligned with my life's purpose to make the world better by starting with one.

As I reflect back on my story, I have said to my wife, "I wish I had gotten to where I am faster. Imagine where I could have gotten?" She is always wonderful about reminding me that at least I did get there, always striving and always climbing. My journey allowed me to interact with many dentists who aspire to be more than average as well as many dentists who have incredible skill sets, yet they struggle with the same challenges I had early in my career.

My purpose in writing this book and for my coaching work is to help dentists accelerate their journeys to reach more and higher peaks than they would otherwise. My journey was mine, and your journey will be yours. I have written this book very intentionally to give you tools to fix how you think about yourself and your practice, with specific action steps to achieve forward progress. This book is meant to be read and reread since some concepts and ideas will apply at different points in your career. Be sure to check out my website at www.UltimateSuccess.Dentist, where I offer more leadership guidance, free templates, and worksheets to guide you through exercises in this book.

If you do what I suggest, you will see yourself grow. You will feel your confidence mount, and you'll see your team, patients, and other relationships change. There is no turning back—nor would you want to. Go ahead with full force to become all you know you are capable of. ⚑

PART I

MINDSET

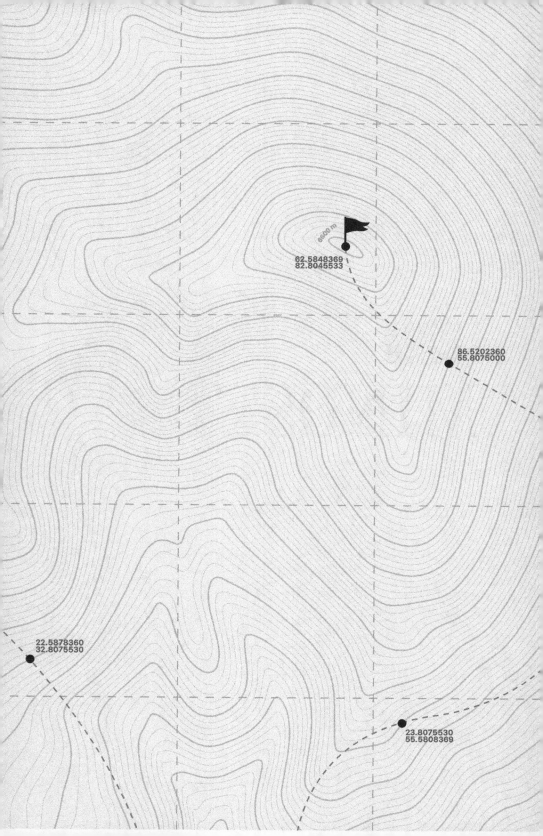

6600 m

62.5848369
82.8045533

86.5202360
55.8075000

22.5878360
32.8075530

23.8075530
55.5808369

CHAPTER 1

Under Your Hood

Things are not always what they seem; the first
appearance deceives many; the intelligence of a few
perceives what has been carefully hidden.

—PHAEDRUS

When you are asked what you think about a certain subject, you likely believe that, in that moment, you actually are thinking about your response. The reality is that you very rarely think about your responses to questions, and many times you don't even process the question. What you believe is true, and how you think about your world has been programmed into your brain's neural circuitry so that you don't even give yourself the opportunity to actually contemplate subjects before you speak. You simply answer. All the experiences and observations in your life have created a template in your subconscious brain. How you respond to your environment is dictated by these templates. You will always default to your subconscious view of the world, whether that viewpoint has been intentionally developed or left to chance.

Notice the difference between your brain's process and the time to respond to the following two questions:

- How do you feel about Donald Trump as a president?

- What is the sum of 467 and 2,179?

The first question you will give very little thought to and respond quickly. For the second question, you will pause and use a different process to actually "think," then come up with your answer. By understanding how our brains work, we can begin to understand ourselves much better.

When I was fifteen years old, I spent part of my day at my father's office to observe him in action. Though the concept of "shadowing" hadn't been coined at that time, I was observing him to see if I wanted to be a civil engineer, as he was. I already felt I was interested in dentistry, yet my parents and I both thought I would benefit by exploring engineering as a potential future profession. My father had been promoted to the highest level possible in the New York State Department of Transportation system, sitting just beneath the politically appointed positions. He no longer spent his days in the field looking at jobs. People reported to him on projects, and he was accountable for the outcome of many intrastate highways and bridge construction projects in New York State. As I observed him that day, I quickly got bored because all I saw him do was paperwork and occasionally answer the phone.

Halfway through the morning, a man rather forcefully pushed past my father's secretary and barged into my father's office. To set the stage, my father was all of five feet and weighed 120 pounds, while this construction worker was close to six feet tall, all muscle, weighing over two hundred pounds. This man walked toward my father's desk and, without saying hello, said, "Are you tracking my work hours?"

My father calmly stood up, came around his desk, and positioned himself right in front of this man. To me, it looked like David and Goliath. "Yes, Robert, I am."

"Why?"

"Well, Robert, I notice that you regularly submit overtime hours, and at the same time, I notice your car missing from the parking lot when I leave each day. I'm curious how you can still be at work, yet the car you drove to work is gone at the end of your regular, non-overtime day? What are your thoughts on that, Robert?" Robert had nothing to say. In that moment, his anger subsided considerably, and he assumed a less threatening body posture. He turned and walked out of the room.

My palms were sweaty, and I imagine I was shaking a little. My father seemed calm as he went back to his desk and continued with his work. Later that day, I asked him about the incident. He told me he didn't know Robert well but knew his name and had noticed his car. Though it wasn't my dad's job to check on workers' hours, he was responsible for the entire budget as well as the outcome of the construction itself, so "every little bit mattered." He told me he had become curious about whether Robert was abusing the overtime system, so he began tracking Robert's time card against his actual hours worked.

My father went about gathering facts to determine whether Robert was cheating the system. I asked if he was a little nervous when he confronted this brute face to face. He smiled and said, "At one point in my career, that would have been a difficult confrontation. Back then, I knew I had to become better at those crucial conversations in order to advance up the ranks. I found that people want to know the truth about your intentions. I am simply determining whether Robert is cheating the system. If he is, I will make sure he returns the money and discuss with him what will happen if we have to address this overtime matter again. But I suspect Robert is a good guy who has a family he needs to support, and perhaps he has been making a bad decision that now has become a bad habit. If it turns out he has been misreporting his hours and collecting overtime he is not entitled to, I am confident that after we speak, he will correct his ways. However, I will continue to check in with Robert to let him know I expect him to perform well, and I believe in him and that he will do so." That's leadership in action. Yet my father said he wasn't always that way. I was certainly blessed to be able to witness many examples of my father's leadership skills as I watched him interact with people in many different scenarios. My father was an incredible leader, yet he wasn't born that way. He had spent years training himself to think well. Leadership requires "thinking well" about our responsibility as leaders.

> **Leadership requires "thinking well" about our responsibility as leaders.**

Of course, we all want to jump into a new sports car and feel the power and engineering at 7,000 rpm and that sensation of being glued to the road as we navigate a hairpin turn at high speed. However, unless you're an auto mechanic, you will probably be satisfied just driving the car without ever inspecting or adjusting what makes that machine perform so well.

Our lives are similar in that we put our energy into driving our lives without intentionally learning about the mechanics of everything unseen. You know when you look at a Ford Focus that it isn't a Porsche 718 Cayman GT4 RS, so you would be crazy to jump into the Ford Focus and scream your way into a hairpin turn. But what about your own mind? Have you purposefully examined and fine-tuned the mechanics of what is under your "hood" to achieve top performance? Are you intentional at creating the racing machine of your mind so it will allow you to achieve all you are meant to be? Let's explore this world together and find the keys to the accelerant that will move you faster toward your life goals and purpose.

I want to suggest to you that everything you have become and will become is totally under your control, and the control is found in the 5.5 inches between your left and right ear—your brain. I'm certain that the idea of thoughts coming from your brain *is not new to you*. However, I am certain that for most people, the idea that your thoughts determine everything you are or will become *is a new one*. This inspection of thoughts and my position on thought are at the core of this book, determining your life and everything good or bad that will happen to you.

History teaches us that many individuals have contributed to our understanding of the human mind. In the fifth century BC, Socrates established the idea that you cannot depend on the authorities to have the correct insight and knowledge to solve your issues.[1] He showed how just because an individual is in a powerful political position does not mean they have the answers for you. Each of us

---

1   Richard Kraut, "Socrates," britannica.com, July 26, 1999, https://www.britannica.com/biography/Socrates.

needs to ask deep questions that are intended to probe into our own mind to determine what the truth is. Within his framework, we see the importance of looking for evidence and of carefully examining commonly held reasoning and general assumptions held by those around us. The examination and questioning of these commonly held beliefs and assumptions may very well lead you to discover that no matter how appealing and comforting they may initially feel to us, following the path laid out by common thinking may not have adequate factual support and may not be congruent with the path you want your practice and your life to take. Today, Socrates's concept of probing your own mind for the right way of thinking is called Socratic questioning.[2]

Socrates was followed by Plato and Aristotle, whose teachings emphasize that things are often very different from what they appear to be and that you must train your mind to look beyond what appears to be the truth on the surface, to see how things really are.

As a practical example, my daughter, Dr. Cassandra Murphy, decided to pursue setting up a scratch practice since she had been unsuccessful at locating a GP dental practice for sale within seventy-five miles of her community. Common thinking guided her to hire a company for a fee of $50,000 that specialized in start-up dental practices. She was told that they were "the experts," and they came highly recommended by other dentists who had used them for their own "start-from-scratch" dental offices. Their methods were exactly what you might expect—use the least costly materials possible to perform the leasehold build-out, participate with all insurance policies, consider participating in Medicaid, and understand that doing a $400

2   Francesca Forsythe, "What Is Socratic Questioning and How to Use It for Self-Analysis and Problem-Solving," learning-mind.com, April 16, 2018, https://www.learning-mind.com/socratic-questioning/.

crown as a participating dentist is better than the "obvious alternative" of twiddling your thumbs and doing nothing. Their expectation was for her to become profitable in twelve months.

To her credit, she watched the conventional model as it began to unfold and realized it did not fit with her vision. Conventional wisdom was either incorrect or a poor match for her goals and her purpose as a dentist. She chalked up the start-up company as a learning opportunity and redirected her practice to a fee-for-service model that focused on relationships and high-quality patient experiences. By her second month in this business, she was profitable and receiving an income.

Bad Thinking Habits

In the sixteenth century, Sir Francis Bacon laid out his position in his book *The Advancement of Learning*. In his works, he found that the human mind cannot be safely left to its own natural tendencies. That tendency is to display a confident, "shiny coat" on the outside while simultaneously having a very confused understanding of ourselves and self-contradictory beliefs. His work laid much of the foundation for modern science with emphasis on the information-gathering process. He developed what he called "idols," which represent the bad-thinking habits that humans pick up. He identified several different types of idols, most notably the "Idols of the Theatre," which represent our tendency to become trapped in conventional schools of thought, and "Idols of the Schools," the poor-thinking habits that develop when our instruction comes from blind rules or poor instruction.

Today, many years since your dental school learning, can you see that you fell prey to accepting that instruction as ideal and proper? Now, through continuing education, you have been exposed to a different level and method of clinical evaluation, optimal diagnosis, and complete dental care, and you realize that much of what you were taught in dental school was wrong for you, so it doesn't apply to how you want to treat your patients or run your dental business.

Sir Francis Bacon was followed by notable philosophers and scientists such as Descartes, Machiavelli, Voltaire, and Sir Isaac Newton. All these individuals added to what is now considered critical thinking, and despite the different additions they each made, they all held the same common belief: for thinking to be critical, ideas must not be accepted at face value. We must all analyze and assess all concepts for their accuracy, clarity, and relevance to our goals and desires. Therefore, by its very nature, all reasoning can be biased by points of view and frames of reference, and you must take great care when you are interpreting the data at hand.

Some of the questions you should consider when you are faced with a decision are as follows:

- What is the real issue here?

- From what point of view should I approach this issue?

- Am I making any unfounded assumptions?

- Am I making any quick and perhaps unsupported inferences?

- Is my train of thought consistent throughout the decision-making process?

- What makes this question complex?

- How can I simplify this issue into its central theme?

- How can I check the accuracy of these "facts"?

- If this is true, what else is implied?

- Do I have credible sources for my information?

Fifteen years into my fee-for-service dental business, my good friend Steve and I spent a weekend together at his lake house. We had lots of time to work together on his lake house projects and discuss life issues. At one point, as I was casually grousing about the past week, Steve asked me to explain the source of my frustrations. I shared my all-too-common story that during the prior week, my number-one assistant was out of the office on one of her three weeks of vacation. Consequently, I was performing many procedures with another assistant who was neither familiar with the procedure nor familiar with working with me. After a number of probing questions from Steve, I realized that there were "elephant-sized" questions I had never thought to ask. That was: When one team member is out of the office for their vacation time or personal days, does the office function as well as when the person is there? If the office does function as well, is that because that team member or that position isn't needed? Or when a team member is out of the office, does the team's ability to function diminish due to the team and the doctor feeling stressed? Do certain tasks get dropped because there isn't enough "people power" to provide the same experience as when we are fully staffed?

The obvious answer for me was that for my lean team of five, when one team member wasn't there, the team felt stressed. Even though the other team members worked at picking up the slack, they were stressed, and patients experienced us at less than our best. I told Steve there wasn't an alternative and that was just the way dentistry was. He helped me see how ingrained my way of thinking had become. Was there a solution? Perhaps not for you, but for me, it was a resounding *yes*. After that weekend chat with Steve, my team and I never saw patients again unless every team member was in the office. No more personal days or individual team member vacation time. I'm happy to provide the reader with more details about the logistics of this shift, but our "Noble Purpose," wanting to be our best when we were with patients, was one large step closer to fulfillment.

Aside from being able to think critically when you are making decisions or processing information, we all need to be aware of the Head Trash™ that has become ingrained in our thinking process and therefore reflected in the results we experience. Your understanding of how you look at the world is critical to achieving your life goals. You must explore the concept of mindset, or how you see the world, and present an argument that helps you realize that how you choose to view the world will be the greatest determinant in the plans you make, the actions you take, and the outcomes you observe in your life.

People have been studying and writing about the power of the mind for millennia. Whatever happens in your life, do you believe that you either have complete control or very little control over the outcomes? The way you answer that question will determine how your entire life plays out. That may sound like a strong statement, and at first, I would agree.

However, depending on what you have read, the people you surround yourself with, and your life experiences, you may or may not believe that if you can dream something in your mind, you can make it come to be. If you knew that you have control over your life outcomes, and you knew what that process looks like, would you choose to live your life by design? I am sure you answered yes, so let's roll up our sleeves, look under your hood, run some diagnostic tests, and fix your bad thinking.

Primitive Creatures

In the 1960s, Paul MacLean, an American neuroscientist, proposed the triune brain model,[3] which divided the human brain into three distinct regions. His model suggests that our brains are organized into an evolutionary hierarchy based on development. The three regions in his model are as follows:

- The reptilian brain (the basal ganglia)

- The emotional brain (the limbic system)

- The rational brain (the neocortex)

His model suggests that as man evolved, so did his brain, and in this manner, the basal ganglia formed first. The basal ganglia is thought to be in charge of our most primal instincts, followed by the limbic system, which is in charge of our emotions, and finally the neocortex, which is responsible for our thought processes. His model suggests that each of these three brain regions operates relatively independent of the other two. Therefore, when we sense we are in danger and must respond very quickly, our reptilian brain is engaged and prepares us for action by initiating the release of certain chemicals in our body, most notably adrenaline. If we witness something upsetting or receive upsetting or exciting news, our limbic system is stimulated, and chemicals are released that create our emotional experience. Lastly, the neocortex shows excited brain activity when we are solving problems or involved in critical thinking (e.g., solving a math problem).

---

3   "A Theory Abandoned but Still Compelling," medicine.yale.edu, September
     15, 2008, https://medicine.yale.edu/news/yale-medicine-magazine/
     article/a-theory-abandoned-but-still-compelling/.

MacLean's model does a nice job of showing us the three different regions of the brain, though today we understand those three areas much better, and we know that they do not act independently of each other. It is much more like a symphony orchestra where different instruments switch in and out from prominent to background, and it is that blending that creates the pleasing musical piece you enjoy. In the brain, all three regions jump in at different times and with different magnitudes, and the final outcome is determined by the interactions and input from all three regions.

Often, we don't think about the reptilian brain since it is more the reactive brain. You can imagine the poor outcome that would occur if you had to "think what to do" when you are right in the path of a moving car! It would be absurd to think that our reaction involves a cognitive thought process such as, "I see a car that is bearing down on me at approximately fifty-five miles per hour, and I suspect, at its current speed and direction, that I will feel impact in 1.5 seconds, at which time I will be hurled into the air approximately 180 feet and …" Of course, the actual response is that you jump out of the way as fast as you can without thinking about it and with more speed and power than you would normally be capable of.

You can thank your basal ganglia and adrenaline for saving your life.

We are all intentionally wired to look for danger and negativity much more than to look for opportunity or pleasant stimuli. Again, you likely don't think about it, yet for a primitive cave dweller, their very survival was dictated by their ability to stay alert and look out for a predatory saber-toothed tiger who would love to eat a caveman for lunch. Every rustle in the bushes might be an opportunity for a meal, but the brain focuses on the negative thought that the rustle could be a predator waiting to end the caveman's life. Science has taught us that this portion of our brain cannot determine what the source of fear is that we are encountering; it only knows that we are experiencing something that is creating the fear response and subsequent adrenaline release. The caveman had the saber-toothed tiger, and we have the protective grizzly-bear sow with her cubs. However, we don't confront or even have to think about being ambushed and killed on a daily basis.

That said, consider this scenario. You see yourself as someone who doesn't like confrontation, and you know you need to speak with one of your team members, Kathy, about her behavior in the office. Kathy will frequently interrupt other team members in your meetings, and when someone even suggests that she doesn't allow others to speak, she pushes back, often with a raised voice, an angry tone, and defensive body language. As you think about telling Kathy that you want to chat, you feel your palms sweat and your heart rate increase.

You aren't even speaking with Kathy, yet just thinking about the upcoming chat creates this response. You expect that the chat will become confrontational, which makes your body sense that you are under attack. The subsequent basal ganglia response and adrenaline release create your physiologic changes (sweating palms and elevated heart rate). Of course, you aren't going to die or be killed simply by having a chat with Kathy! However, your brain is somehow convinced this is a life-threatening event, and it reacts accordingly.

The Amygdala

This phenomenon has been called "amygdala hijacking," and the phrase was first used by psychologist Daniel Goleman in his 1995 book *Emotional Intelligence: Why It Can Matter More Than IQ*. Amygdala hijacking refers to an immediate and intense emotional reaction that's out of proportion to the present situation. In other words, it's when someone "loses it" or seriously overreacts to something or someone. While the amygdala is intended to protect us from danger, it can interfere with our functioning in the modern world, where threats are often more subtle in nature. Or, as in the example above, it can create a reaction to a situation that hasn't even occurred. It is just a scenario that you are playing in your head, yet the scenario feels so real to your brain that it reacts just as if you are really under attack and your life is in danger.[4]

I remember early in my career when I hired a consultant to help me run my office. Of course, I was the problem, but I was still early in my journey, and I couldn't understand why my team wouldn't do what I asked them to do. My consultant, Robert, told me that my homework for the coming week was to sit down with my patient coordinator, Lynn, and discuss why she was not following through with certain tasks in her daily routine. I spoke with Robert each Friday at 1:00 p.m. After our Friday call, I told myself that I would speak with Lynn first thing Monday morning. The thought of having to confront Lynn on Monday made for a long and nervous weekend. When Monday morning came, I was so worked up internally that "there was no way I could talk to her today." I found a million reasons to procrastinate talking with Lynn until finally it was Friday morning. I respected Robert too much to let him down, so I spoke with Lynn. I am sure the conversation didn't go well, but we spoke. When Robert and I spoke at 1:00 p.m. that day, he immediately asked if I had spoken with Lynn, and I said I had. His first reply was, "And you didn't die, did you?" I learned a little more that day about how powerful my brain was and whether it was helping me or stopping me. For me and you, often when our brain reacts like we are under attack, it is

---

4   Daniel Goleman, *Emotional Intelligence: Why It Can Matter More Than IQ* (New York, NY: Random House, 2005).

more likely just an uncomfortable feeling that is being magnified by our limbic system.

Fear

At the heart of amygdala hijacking is fear. Some not-so-jokingly say that fear is an acronym for "false evidence appearing real" (FEAR). Aside from the grizzly sow with cubs and the speeding car bearing down on you at close range, most other fears are actually doubts that get magnified into all-out fear. Fear is defined by Merriam-Webster as "an unpleasant often strong emotion caused by anticipation or awareness of danger." Fear causes changes in how we think, which in turn produces behavioral reactions. These reactions have been bundled into catchy phrases: fight or flight, freeze or appease. Fear in human beings may occur in response to certain stimuli occurring in the present. The fear response arises from the perception of danger, leading to confrontation with or escape from the threat. This response is also known as the fight-or-flight response, which in extreme cases of fear (horror or terror) can be a freeze response or paralysis.

So that's fear. What do I call what I experienced when I had to confront Lynn in my dental-office scenario described earlier? Rather than terming that experience as fear, I am better off defining it as anxiety. Anxiety is defined by Merriam-Webster as "apprehensive uneasiness or nervousness usually over an impending or anticipated ill." Anxiety is often accompanied by muscular tension, restlessness, fatigue, inability to catch one's breath, tightness in the abdominal region, nausea, and problems with concentration.

Anxiety is certainly closely related to fear, with the difference being that fear is a response to a real or perceived threat that is occurring right now, whereas anxiety is the feeling associated with the expectation of a future threat. So for me, thinking about having to confront my patient coordinator, Lynn, was causing me anxiety over the course of the week, and then when I was actually sitting in front of her and getting ready to speak, that was fear.

For our purposes, we combine fear and anxiety into one bucket since they both can interfere with you making the right decision and choosing the right action. Your fears come from your own experiences as well as the fears we acquire vicariously by observing others. A common fear transmission is from a parent to a child. The child repeatedly observes their parent's fear regarding a particular situation, and they unknowingly become fearful as well. Another source of fear is by association. You may have had an incident in your life, such as when you climbed up on the playground swing set and then fell off. Later on in life, you notice how you have "always had a fear of heights," though you couldn't quite figure out why or when that began. A final and common source of acquired fear is hearing about situations that are fearful to others. Certainly, in all my travels, I have met people who have never flown, but they are deathly afraid of flying because they focus on the extremely rare flight accident that is sensationalized by the media. All these fears and anxieties result in our brain seeing the world as something it is not and creating a reaction that isn't helpful or appropriate.

Deserve Level™

We would be remiss if, in any conversation about our brain creating a false image of what is real, we didn't discuss the concept of Deserve Level™. Our Deserve Level™ consists of the limits we set for ourselves, and these limits act as the comfort range in which we see ourselves; therefore, they dictate our decisions and our commitment to those decisions. I could say, "I deserve to be the wealthiest human on earth," yet if I don't truly believe that to my core, then I really don't feel I deserve it. Your Deserve Level™ is how you see yourself through the lens of your subconscious mind, which is where the ultimate control resides for all your thoughts and actions.

Deserve Level™ is about everything you have—and don't have. Put simply, it's what you believe you're worthy of having, whether it's how much money is in your bank account, the job you have (and either hate or love), the relationship you're in (or not), how your body looks, even the clothes you wear and the house you live in.

You might be saying "Hey, I'm a good person. I deserve to have a business that inspires me every day and pays me an incredible salary." Or perhaps you think, "I have studied and worked hard at building my clinical skill set, and I deserve to be treating more patients and to have more patients say yes to my treatment recommendations."

> **Deserve Level™ is about everything you have—and don't have. Put simply, it's what you believe you're worthy of having.**

If you don't have those things that you feel you deserve, a contributing factor (and I will be so bold as to say the main reason) is that you have a low Deserve Level™ in those areas—deep down where it counts, you don't believe you're worthy of having those very things. Let me rephrase that sentence. Your Deserve Level™ may not be "low"; it is just lower than the item you say you deserve.

Consider that your mind is like a computer's internal operating system. Your decisions about who you are have been unconsciously formed from all your past experiences, and those experiences are what define your Deserve Level™. It's the programming of your subconscious mind that is real yet invisible. There are certain things that you can imagine having, but you simply can't get. That's because you have an unconscious tolerance range that your subconscious mind locks into. If you actually acquire anything outside your Deserve Level™, you'll find a way to sabotage yourself because of your low Deserve Level™ in that area.

Think about the lottery winner who manages to have none of the money in just a few years. How does that happen? The individual is given the money, by luck. They have never seen themselves as a wealthy person, so they don't know how a wealthy person thinks about money. They see themselves as someone who is living paycheck to paycheck, since that is what they have always done. It isn't that the money magically disappears. No, there is a paper trail of where it went. It just went out of this person's life because they could not see themselves as wealthy, only as living paycheck to paycheck. They made decisions that put them right back in that very comfortable and familiar place—living paycheck to paycheck.

Think about the person who gets rapidly promoted up the corporate ladder, only to crash and burn in short order. Or the business owner who, despite a stellar product or service and superb marketing, barely manages to turn a profit. How about a friend of yours who's been married multiple times? They complain about certain characteristics found in their current mate. They get divorced and then marry someone who has many of the same unwanted traits as the first mate.

All of these are prime examples of how the person's subconscious Deserve Level™ is lower than what they say they deserve. If none of these examples ring true for you, consider a sport you play that is dependent solely on your individual performance. Examples are numerous, some of which are such as golf, racket sports, skiing, crew (single), surfing, and bowling. Many of these sports are measured with very specific scores and even handicaps, which essentially define how well you usually perform at this sport.

Here is a common scenario built around Deserve Level™. You love golf, and you usually have a score of 84 with a 12 handicap. You are playing an eighteen-hole round of golf, and after the first nine holes, you are even par, much better than you normally play. As you begin the last nine, you can feel a pressure building up inside you, a voice that says, "You're playing way better than you usually do" and "If you keep this up, you'll have your best score ever." To the outside observer, your play would look different, as you're taking more time for each shot than you did on the first nine holes.

You seem a little irritable, and when you hit a poor shot, your reaction is stronger than you would normally react. After six of the last nine holes have been played, you have played so poorly that now it looks like you'll end up with a score in the low 80s, right in line with your handicap and how you subconsciously see yourself as a golfer. That is how you sabotage yourself—by allowing your subconscious thoughts to tell you that you don't deserve to play as well as you have been because, after all, "that is not how you play." That is not how you "see yourself," and therefore you don't deserve a great score.

Deserve Level™ works the other way as well. Back to a golf example. Let's say you play the first nine holes horribly, and you hear a voice inside your head (and maybe you say it out loud) saying, "This isn't like me—I'm a much better player than this" or "You aren't playing the way you usually do—you always play better than this." Like the first example, but in reverse, when you get to the second nine holes, you become more relaxed because, after all, "this round of golf is going to be horrible." Your usual game returns, and sometimes you'll play better than usual on the last nine because your brain knows that a final score around 84 is how you play—it is how you define yourself as a golfer. More than any other single factor, Deserve Level™ is the determiner of what you accomplish or what you have in every area of your life. It's the unseen force corralling your life, for better or worse.

Key concept: More than any other single factor, Deserve Level™ is the determiner of what you accomplish or what you have in every area of your life. It's the unseen force shaping your life, for better or worse.

I have identified anatomical brain systems and their chemical releases, which result in your "reactive" behavior. We have also identified destructive behavioral patterns that are functions of your brain taking over your thinking. Are you at the mercy of these systems, a victim waiting to be struck by the villainous forces in your head, or can you exert control over them? The good news is that it most certainly can be changed. How do we know? Well, let's think about it.

When you were born, did you have a 12 handicap in golf? No.

When you first picked up a golf club, were you somehow assigned a 12 handicap? No. Have you always had a 12 handicap? No. It was much higher at some point, and then you played and practiced, and you became a better player, and your handicap went down to 12. You may argue, "Well, my ability level is only as good as a 12-handicap player plays." Let's examine that. If that is true, how do you explain the first nine holes when you played to the equivalent of a 2 handicap? Then on the last nine holes, you played so poorly you ended up near your 12 handicap.

What happens if we combine the two golf examples into one round of golf? In the first example, you played the first nine really well (for you), and in the second example, you played the last nine holes really well (for you). So if you combine those two nine-hole rounds into the same eighteen-hole round of golf, you would have scored an incredibly low score for you. But that didn't happen and usually doesn't. Occasionally, you'll "play over your head" and have a great score, and then the next time you are out playing, you're right back to the 12-handicap score or a little worse. Of course, the golf course, your clubs, shoes, balls, tees, etc. have not changed from day to day. The only thing that has changed is how you see yourself as a golfer and how you self-correct to sabotage (when you're doing well) or improve (when you're doing poorly) based on your current state.

So how does that play out in business? In every way imaginable. Here is a short list:

- How do you see yourself as a leader? Does your team follow you? Do you command their respect because of who you are?

- Do patients usually accept your treatment recommendations or not?

- How do you feel when you start to present treatments that have a much higher fee than you ever quoted before? Tight stomach, sweaty palms, increased heart rate?

- Should you invest heavily in your business, or do you worry with thoughts like "But what if ..."?

- A dentist in your town provides essentially the same services you do, yet they take off much more time than you do, drive a really nice car, have nice clothes, and live in the big house. How do they do it when you can't?

I hope you look at these situations with an open mind that asks, "Could this really be true? Am I the actual barrier to my own further success?" Yes indeed, my friend, and it is true for every one of us. All dentists are trained to appreciate the sympathetic nervous system and the fight, flight, freeze, or appease response that we just spoke about. When you are presenting a treatment plan to a patient and your heart rate increases, and your palms are sweaty or clammy cold, that is your limbic system taking over. Why has it been activated? Are you under attack? No. Then what? You are out of your Deserve Level™ to present this much dentistry to this person; the anxiety or fear response kicks in, and your body reacts accordingly.

Nothing more and nothing less. At a very real level, it isn't that you don't think the patient deserves the treatment—it's that you feel that you don't deserve to be the one who does the work for them and gets paid the fee you are asking. It is just that simple. ⚑

KEY TAKEAWAYS

- Your brain is in charge of keeping you alive, so it will look for the negative in the world much more than the positive.
- Most modern-day situations are uncomfortable, not life-threatening, even though our brains respond as if we are under attack.

ACTION STEPS

- Your mind creates the direction your life will take through your senses. Cut or copy pictures that are examples of what you want to achieve in your life, then attach them to the walls in your workplace. Place them where you "accidentally" see them throughout your day. If you want a good marriage and family, put up pictures of a couple holding hands or a laughing family on the beach. You want wealth? Put up images of wealth like yachts, private jets, amazing homes, expensive jewelry, or pictures of gold bars and piles of money.

- As you lie down in bed and feel yourself getting sleepy, create images in your mind of all the good outcomes you want in your life, and literally see yourself using and enjoying them. See yourself in a loving relationship, feel the joy in your heart, feel the crisp air as you ski in the Alps, picture yourself walking across the tarmac to your private jet, or feel the cold and rough edges on your buttocks as you sit alone at the K2 summit. Whatever inspires you to greatness, intentionally let your mind create those images as you drift off to sleep every night.

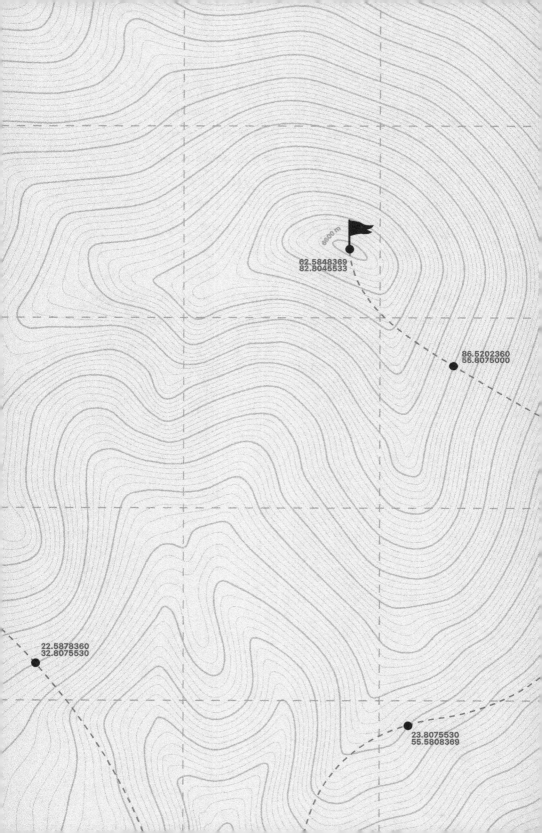

CHAPTER 2

Intentional Thought

*If you can imagine it, you can achieve it. If
you can dream it, you can become it.*

—WILLIAM ARTHUR WARD

We have identified our enemy. We don't apply critical thinking to
our decisions, and even if we did, we sabotage our efforts by allowing
ourselves to be held hostage by our fears, anxieties, and closely held
beliefs about ourselves. By combining these throughout every moment
of our waking day, we subconsciously sabotage ourselves. All this,
simply because we do not know how to see ourselves as worthy of the
outcome or goals we desire. These actions and thoughts dictate the
thinking patterns and responses that create how we see and react to
the world.

So how do you defeat the enemy? Overcoming your fears and anxieties is a lifelong journey. We all have our share of demons disrupting our thought processes. Clinical psychology has multiple types of therapy that include psychoanalytical therapy and cognitive behavioral therapy. You'll have to decide when your fears and anxieties are getting in your way so much that you decide to hire a therapy coach who will work with you. With the right therapist, you can hope to achieve great and long-lasting progress.

Envision First

As you explore how your thoughts affect your actions and therefore your life, you'll likely run into books like *As a Man Thinketh*, by James Allen, or *The Science of Getting Rich*, by Wallace Wattles. These books help the reader understand that there is a simple (but not easy) process to achieve anything you want. First, in your mind you must envision whatever you want, and that vision must include all the details of that thing—what it looks like, feels like, smells like, and tastes like. Use all your senses.

Belief/Faith

You must believe to the core of your being that you deserve that thing and believe that thing is going to come into your life. That belief may be without any proof whatsoever that the thing you desire will ever appear. That 100 percent belief in something we cannot see, touch, taste, or hear is called faith. These authors, and so many individuals before and after them, have described how faith and faith alone will allow you to acquire anything that you conceive in your mind. If it is that simple, why doesn't everyone have whatever they want? Great question. It is that simple, but it is not that easy. Changing how you see yourself or how you see those around you can be very difficult and requires complete commitment.

Zero Proof

Tiger Woods, the golfing great, was awarded the single largest endorsement Nike had ever offered an athlete, even before Tiger had won his first professional golf tournament. That's right. Tiger received the single largest endorsement that Nike had ever paid any athlete in any sport, and Tiger hadn't won a single professional tournament yet. Why would Nike do that? Nike said that they could feel the energy in Tiger, and they were convinced that when he told them he would become the greatest golfer in golfing history, that he believed it so completely that he would make it happen. And he did! If you watch Olympic gymnasts and divers, just prior to their performances, you'll often see them making small movements and gyrations as they visualize every single movement of their upcoming event—they can see it so clearly in their mind that their body just must follow that and perform. Many Olympic medalists talk about how they could feel the weight of the gold medal hanging around their neck years before they won an event because their faith was so complete.

Faith is often thought of in a spiritual or religious context, and even then, it means having complete trust or confidence in someone or something in the absence of any proof. If you are a spiritual being, then you are familiar with having faith in a God or Supreme Being. That said, even an atheist has faith—a true atheist has 100 percent belief that there isn't a God or gods. My point is that we all have faith in something, and the point of this discussion is for you to accept, as faith, that you can make changes and become a different dentist, owner, leader, and being, and by virtue of those changes, the practice you envision will come to fruition, one step at a time. Your process will be much like the captain of a ship who is setting sail across the ocean to a destination he cannot see. He knows where he wants to go. He knows there will be storms at sea and pressures that may suggest he should stop the trip or go back to safety, yet the knowing captain will trust his crew, ship, and instruments and have complete faith that they will reach the exact destination they set out to reach.

For the purpose of this book, I want to introduce you to a simple technique to enable you to catch yourself when you are slipping into a less-than-positive-and-helpful mindset. This is a step-by-step method that will allow you to move yourself through your fears/anxieties and raise your Deserve Level™ so you perform as a much better version of yourself.

Tell Yourself a Different Story

How do you change your Deserve Level™ so it levels up to what you want in every area of your life? There is no single pathway to success, but I will help you find one that works for you.

Consider that you likely have a higher Deserve Level™ in some areas of your life than others. Examine the inconsistencies in your success over different aspects of your life. Look at where you have high success (as you see it), and pay attention to how you think about that area of your life.

Self-Talk: Your Best Friend or Your Worst Enemy

Most importantly, pay close attention to your self-talk. Each of us talks to ourselves. That is normal. It is the story you say to yourself that counts, as well as what you do right after you hear yourself talking to yourself and speaking poorly about yourself. You'll want to start saying things like the following:

- "Every patient I present treatment to says yes!"

- "I have the most amazing dental team members who are all engaged and pushing for excellence."

- "I am an amazing leader with great employees and great patients, and financial rewards are attracted to me."

This self-talk can also be displayed around you with little Post-it notes that are reminding and encouraging you.

Understand that you'll always have negative self-talk since all humans do. When you hear yourself saying negative things to yourself, stop and say a positive affirming statement. You can't stop the negative self-talk—no one can—but you can control what happens right after the negative self-talk occurs.

For example: You present a full mouth optimal plan to a patient, and they say no. You catch yourself saying, "Of course they said no; all my patients say no to big treatment." Now you can tell yourself something positive, *but* it must be true. You could say, "But every future patient will say yes to big treatment." Given your past record when a few patients said

> **When you are trying to improve your actions, you'll find believable examples of how you are getting better—tell yourself a true story about that progress.**

yes, it is unlikely that you will believe what you just said. That will not prove beneficial.

Start with small, positive steps that you believe and know are true. You could say to yourself, "Well, the patient didn't say yes, but I know using pictures is helpful, and I showed that patient pictures better than I ever did before" or "I know I need to expect that some or many patients will initially say no to the proposed treatment, but that *no* doesn't necessarily mean no. 'No' often means they just don't know enough about why they should say yes, so today, I moved a little further down that path when I stayed engaged after they said no." Whatever it is, when you are trying to improve your actions, you'll find believable examples of how you are getting better—tell yourself a true story about that progress.

How to Catch Yourself with Unproductive Thoughts

So we agree the mind is a most amazing and powerful energy source, and therefore it needs to be harnessed to make the practice you envision come to life. How do you know if your mind is working with you or against you? Is there a barometer of sorts to let you know? The good news is yes, and it is the way you are feeling right in the moment. You have a vision of your incredible success, and by all the powers of the universe, you are entitled to achieve that vision. You still need to do the work, but you deserve the vision you can see for yourself and your dental business.

When your thoughts are aligned with the vision of success, you will feel at peace with the world; you'll feel confident, energized, and at one with yourself. However, when you notice you are not feeling emotionally well, it is because your thoughts, in that moment, are not aligned with the vision you have set for yourself. Anytime you are feeling negative or poorly emotionally, it is your current thoughts that are creating that lack of harmony. When you notice you are feeling poor emotionally, pay attention to that feeling, and immediately tell yourself a different story, the one you want to come true.

Key concept: Tell yourself the story you want to come true, not the story you don't want to come true.

Change your thoughts, and you change how you feel. Hard to believe? I will prove it to you. Recall a time when you had recently done a lot of work on a patient, and then a few days later, you see on your schedule that they are coming in for an emergency visit. Does your brain race to "I bet they are coming in to tell me how fantastic the dentistry is and how they cannot thank me enough"? Or does your self-talk sound more like "Oh no, there must be something wrong with the dentistry I just did; I wonder what broke or doesn't look good"? If your thoughts go immediately to congratulating yourself, good for you, and keep it up. Most of the hundreds, or even thousands, of dentists I have been around in the last forty years have a version of the second story: something is wrong with the dentistry you just did, and the patient isn't happy.

Prior to seeing the patient's name in your schedule, you feel fine. Then, right when you see their name, see how your emotions change from good to bad. You might suddenly feel a pit in your stomach, and your heart rate increases a little. The patient arrives at your office, and when you see them, they say, "Doc, the dentistry you did feels great, but the other area we didn't get to yet is starting to crumble. What do you suggest we do?" How do you feel now? Suddenly, the story in your head is a positive one, and immediately your emotions went to feeling good—just like that! Change your thoughts, and you will change your emotional state.

Begin noticing how you feel in any given moment. When you feel bad emotionally, it will be because you are telling yourself a story that you *do not* want to happen. You didn't want your dentistry to be broken or look poor, and when you thought it did, you got a pit in your stomach. When the real reason the patient came in as an emergency was known, and you know they love what you did and they want your advice on another part of their mouth, your story changed to positive—"I am a good dentist, this patient really likes the work I did, they want me to do more, and they trust me." Immediately, the pit in your stomach goes away, and a smile radiates through your body.

In their book *Money and the Law of Attraction*, Esther and Jerry Hicks identify that while you may not be able to figure out what to do that will make you feel better, you always know how you want to feel. When you feel upset with a pit in your stomach, you recognize that, and you know you want to feel relaxed and calm.

If you understand the power of your thought and the incredible leverage that consistently good-feeling thoughts provide, and you begin deliberately choosing your thoughts by utilizing the guidance that your feelings or emotions indicate, you can easily transform your life into predominantly good-feeling experiences by focusing on the improved feeling. If you are able to find even the smallest feeling of relief in a deliberately chosen thought, your gentle path toward your solution will begin.[5]

---

5   Esther Hicks and Jerry Hicks, Money, and the Law of Attraction: Learning to Attract Wealth, Health, and Happiness (Carlsbad, CA: Hay House, 2008).

> **Key concept:** Tell yourself the story you want to see come true, and watch yourself begin to feel uplifted and positive.

The expectation of this book is not to completely turn you into a believer of this process. However, by learning to visualize what you want and never giving up on that vision, you'll see the strong correlation between your thoughts and how your business grows and succeeds.

Perhaps the best news is that neuroscience and behavioral science now agree that our brain's nervous system can actually change. We used to think that the brain was "hardwired," meaning that the neural connections, once formed, would never change. Now we know that the nervous system is very adaptable. Science refers to the neural system as neuroplasticity. You experience this neuroplasticity every day, just as when you met someone yesterday and you recall their name today. We now know the nervous system is adaptable and can be intentionally or unintentionally rewired.

> **By learning to visualize what you want and never giving up on that vision, you'll see the strong correlation between your thoughts and how your business grows and succeeds.**

Geneticists refer to the concept of epigenetics. Our experiences can change not only our brains but also even the expression of our genes—or, more precisely, how our genes are expressed. Scientists used to believe that our genes were unchangeable and responsible for most illnesses.

Recently, however, the study of epigenetics has shown that the way our genes are expressed changes in response to our experiences and our external environment. This has led scientists to theorize that only 5 percent of today's illnesses are the result of genes, and the rest are the results of our environment. This could mean that if you experience chronic stress throughout your life, you may be genetically predisposing your future offspring to chronic stress as well and that dealing with stress in a healthy way can benefit your future offspring and subsequent generations. On the other hand, a positive uplifting internal state can help us overcome hurtful and toxic environments, and now many believe we all can change our own gene pools as well as gene pools of future generations, simply by changing our mindset with the thoughts we create and what we focus on. As you sit there with this book in hand or on an e-reader, pay attention to the stories you are telling yourself. Are you telling yourself a story based on past "failures" or a story full of doubt? Are you saying, "That worked for you, but you don't have the challenges I have." As the saying goes, changing the story you tell yourself is simple, but it is not easy. I imagine that at this very moment, you have a thought running through your head to which, if you blurted it out loud and then asked yourself, "Is that the story I want to come true?" you would say *no*. Try it. Listen to your self-talk. Do you hear a story you don't want to come true? If so, immediately tell yourself a story that you believe in—the story you do want to come true. ⚑

KEY TAKEAWAYS

- Left to itself, your brain runs at the subconscious level most of the time, and you actually think very little.
- How we subconsciously "see ourselves" will dictate how we act, and the results will support our subconscious views.

ACTION STEPS

- Pay attention to your emotions and realize that when you experience physical discomfort, you are telling yourself a story you do not want to come true. I am not speaking of physical pain due to an illness but rather about physical discomfort that is directly tied to incorrect self-talk.
- Next time you feel your stomach churning, a slight headache, or overall tension, examine exactly what story you are running through your mind.
- Now that you have identified this story that you *don't want to come true*, tell yourself a story about *what you do want to come true*.
- Each time you feel a gnawing feeling in your gut, examine your thoughts in that moment and identify the bad-outcome story you're telling yourself. Then immediately create a better and believable story that moves you in the direction you want to go.

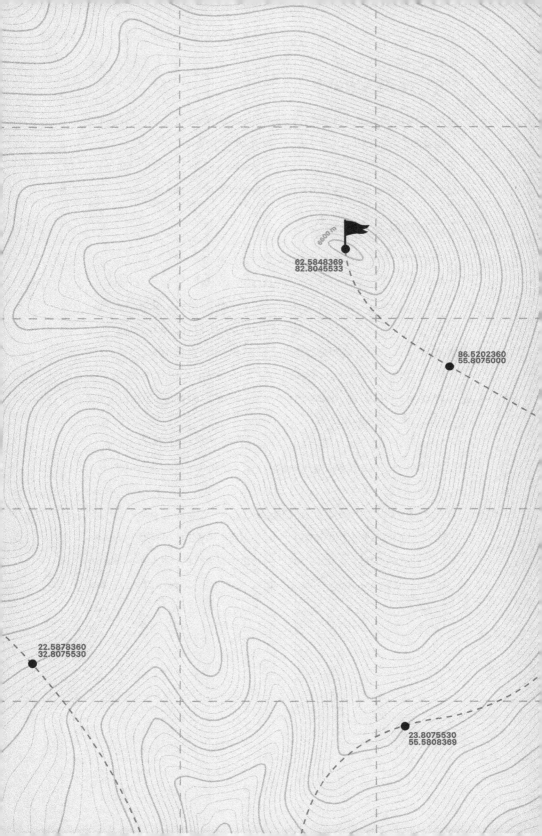

6600 m

62.5848369
82.8045533

86.5202360
55.8075000

22.5878360
32.8075530

23.8075530
55.5808369

CHAPTER 3

Applied Mindset

To know and not to do is not yet to know.

—LAO TZU

Recall the beginning of this book, where I introduced you to my father and the time I witnessed him as an amazing leader. He was the "boss" for many people, yet he wasn't entrepreneurial in any sense of the word. As a matter of fact, he felt business ownership was too risky. He saw being an employee of New York State as the safer path since they would never go out of business. Nonetheless, he had amazing leadership skills and, in that rendition of David and Goliath, my father, a five-foot-tall guy, walked right up to the huge, angry construction worker and confronted him in such a calm, truthful, and respectful manner that the big guy was left speechless and quickly exited the room. Wouldn't you love to have that ability?

I explained how you can learn to think better, then gave you a great mechanism to add a believable story to your self-talk. You bring your mindset with you wherever you go, so let's look at the wonders an improved mindset will create for you.

Recently a dentist approached me when one of his colleagues told him to ask me about the problem he and his partner were encountering. Bill and his partner, Lewis, had practiced together for twenty years. They had created two wonderful practices, producing optimal dentistry with great patient experiences. Lewis wanted to begin taking off large blocks of time, and they couldn't determine how that would be fair to Bill. They had worked out the money part, but the problem, as Bill saw it, was that when Lewis was away from the office, Bill had to be there every day, preventing him from taking off his usual one week every month. I asked Bill why he couldn't take time off. He said that with both dentists out of the office, he wouldn't have a vacation because he would get emails, texts, and calls from his team all day long. He felt he might as well be in the office. I told him that in my office, I worked by myself and closed the office to patient care for twelve to fourteen weeks per year, and I couldn't recall ever getting a call or an email from my team when I was out of the office. If I did, it was a matter that could wait until I returned to the office. My team was trained and very willing to evaluate issues, come up with the possible solutions, and then make their best decision. They did a great job of doing so. Bill looked at me like I had three heads and said, "That would be amazing, but I don't see how that could ever happen." That was his mindset. He felt the only way his office would run was if he or Lewis were there to "make sure things were done right."

Can you picture the grin on Bill's face now when he gets back from a weeklong staycation or vacation and appreciates that his time off wasn't interrupted to solve an office issue? Now his team does it for him, just like he wants them to. My description of another way and his open-mindedness to change the way he viewed his team and created a shift in his mindset. He trained his team and himself to think differently about leadership and who is responsible for what, and his team gladly rose to the occasion. Everyone in Bill and Lewis's office is happier with their new way of thinking about how their office runs.

Virtually all dentists I meet want to work less and make more money. Who wouldn't? How does a mindset shift—changing the way you think and making small steps in the right direction—apply to an ambitious goal of doubling or tripling your office revenue? A difficult aspect of believing that "if you conceive it, you can achieve it" is that sometimes there is a big gap between where you are and where you want to be.

> **Virtually all dentists I meet want to work less and make more money. Who wouldn't?**

As an example, suppose your practice is collecting $700,000 per year, and you understand other offices are collecting four times that while spending less time than you (working less and making more money). You would like that as well, but what does that process to go from $700,000 to $2.8 million look like? The sequence of steps starts with a crystal-clear picture of what the $2.8 million business looks like and then reverse-engineering it—as the saying goes, "eating the elephant one bite at a time."

- First, you'll expand by 50 percent, going from $700,000 per year ($59,000 per month) to $1.5 million per year ($88,000 per month). Using the current number of days per year you work, determine what production you need per day to reach $88,000 per month and then what production per hour is needed to reach the daily goal you just determined. Production per hour is by far the most important *production metric* for you to keep track of. You can always produce more by working more hours. But you said you want to work less and make more money, so focus on production per hour, not overall production per day, week, month, or year.

- Knowing how much you need to increase production each day, look at each clinician's schedule and the procedures each provides, and decide how each clinician can increase their hourly production to reach their new daily and cycle goals.

- Adjust the schedule with block booking so each clinician's schedule will reach the necessary goals.

- Fill in the blocks with patients who want that dental treatment (e.g., to meet the production goal for the day, the doctor's first block of the day must have $2,400, and your fee for crowns is $1,200, so you will only schedule patients who need two crowns or more in that block; do not put anything less productive in that block until the last possible moment). If the time in the schedule isn't blocked off, production will only happen by chance, and it will be very inconsistent.

- Repeat the process every day without getting distracted or inserting more steps.

- Once you are at $1.05 million in revenue, you'll follow the same process and continue looking for ways to maximize your production per patient per hour of work—working smarter, not longer.

Key concept: The longest journey begins with but a single step. Know where you want the practice to go in the distant future. Then determine where it needs to be at time increments along the way. Each of these milestones needs to be measurable and have a written date of completion.

All of us have done this on a road trip. For example, if we are driving from New York to California, we know exactly where we are starting from (our home) and exactly where we are going to (Aunt Mary's home). We pick the most direct route, decide when we want to get there, then we divide the trip up into equal driving hours each day. Notice how all of these legs are predetermined when we know these three vital elements:

- Where exactly are we starting from?

- Where exactly do we want to go?

- How long do we want the trip to take?

Whether it is taking a road trip or growing your business, the concepts are identical. Keep that analogy in mind as you take this journey with your team so that you stay on the plotted course, keep moving forward, and focus on each leg of the trip. The first step is constantly telling yourself the story you want to hear. The value of the above exercise is that you may not see a way to move your production from $700,000 to $2.8 million. It is too big of a leap, so it is difficult to convince yourself it is possible. However, breaking it down into smaller steps allows you to see that if the hygienists do one more sealant per patient or one more soft-tissue procedure per week, they will meet their new daily goals. When you do one more crown per day, you meet your new daily goal. That is much more doable. You tell yourself this story because you believe it; your mindset and your team's mindset just shifted to "We can do this!" The rest is just a matter of diagnosing the work and protecting your block-booked schedule.

Sales Organization Mindset

Perhaps the most difficult mindset to overcome is selling. I expect to provide you with enough content and reasons that you embrace the fact that you are selling something to your patients. In grand terms, you are selling them what they came to you for: your vision for their dental health so that that optimal dental health will give them a better quality of life. *Patient lives improve with optimal dental care.*

I want you to understand and embrace the goodness in helping a patient go through a process of discovery where they *want* the results that optimal dentistry will give them. You are doing them a favor by helping them achieve optimal dental health. Do you believe that? Are you telling yourself that story, or are you telling yourself a story that sounds like "I don't want the patient to think I am trying to sell them something, so I won't push this treatment onto them." There need to be sequential steps that each patient experiences, from the first time they hear about your practice, to the end of their optimal dental care. *Those steps—that process—is called your sales process.* The question is: Do you want to let it happen on its own and by chance? Or do you want to become a master at every step of the process? I hope you choose to become a master of the process.

Let me pose a question to you. Say your practice produces $1 million per year. A patient comes into your office, and you propose $10,000 of optimal dental care for them, which will change their smile and give them all the benefits they can hope for from dentistry. They say *yes* or they say *no*. Who is the biggest winner or biggest loser either way? Well, let's look at that. If the patient says *yes* and gets the work done, they have a truly life-changing experience that they will enjoy for years to come. The office receives $10,000. While that's true, that only represents one percent (1 percent) of the revenue for the year, so it is a relatively small number compared to the total $1 million that needs to be collected for the year. The patient will enjoy the dentistry for years to come, but *the office will not enjoy the $10,000 for very long*. In reality, the office has to immediately create more opportunities with other patients, all of which adds up to the $1 million in annual revenue.

The patient is clearly the biggest winner when they say yes.

What happens when they say no? The business doesn't get the $10,000 from this patient, right? True, but the scheduled time that this patient would have used is still open to put another productive procedure into. Even if that time was never filled, the $10,000 loss is only 1 percent of the office annual revenue. One percent doesn't affect the office in any significant way. However, the patient gets zero improvement in dental health and therefore misses their chance to benefit from life-changing optimal dentistry. I hope you see and agree that the patient is the biggest loser. Therefore, if your business's noble purpose is to help patients, the more you embrace the sales process and master the process of becoming a sales organization, the more you will be able to fulfill your noble purpose.

> **Key concept:** The patient is the big winner when they say yes, and the patient is the big loser when they say no. Help them to say yes.

I offer this example to help you have a good reason why you need to change your mindset around sales. Every time someone buys something, anything, a sale has happened. You might say, "But salespeople have a bad reputation, and I don't want to be thought of as a salesperson." That's fair, so let's take a closer look at what the idea of selling can be and should be.

Let me describe two different scenarios to you, and you tell me which fits your picture of a salesperson.

Scenario 1

I am a salesperson in a car dealership that has two fast and expensive red cars that the dealership wants to move off the lot. If I sell them, I will make a very nice profit, and whoever buys the cars will get a very nice fast car. A young couple walks into the dealership. They are nicely dressed, and I immediately introduce myself. They say they're looking for a fun car, and they point to the two red cars that are certainly very fun to drive and might be fun to be seen in. We have very little conversation about them, and we have a lot of conversation about how this car is just right for them, how fast it is, and how they would look great in the car. We take it out for a test drive, where I point out all the bells and whistles and how this is the best car for them and today; I say we have just two of these cars, so they should decide quickly before they lose the opportunity. They may or may not buy the car.

Scenario 2

I am in the same dealership with the same two fast red cars, and the same sharp young couple walk in. I introduce myself, and we chat for a few moments, and they express an interest in the two fast red cars. I begin to engage the couple with some questions, starting with, "Is it OK if I ask you some questions about your life and how you would use the car?" They agree.

Among other questions, I ask:

- Do you have children, or do you plan on having children?

- Do you care about the resale value of your car?

- Do you have any hobbies that might require towing something behind your car?

- Are you concerned about the overall construction safety of your car in collision tests?

- Are you concerned about the gas mileage that your vehicle has?

- Are you looking for a car that is very fast and can go from zero to 60 mph in less than six seconds?

- How many people do you expect to put in the car at any given time?

- Do you care whether the car is made in the United States?

- Are you looking for a certain car manufacturer?

- How important is the reliability of a particular brand of car?"

Throughout this discovery process, I have one agenda—to find out everything about this couple, their life, how they might use the car, and what is important or not important to them when it comes to car ownership. Why? So that I can make a very specific recommendation for one or two vehicles that will fit into their life and meet their needs and wants as they describe them to me. I will continue to ask open-ended questions that encourage them to elaborate on why certain features in a car are important to them, now and in the near future. If I have done my job well, at the end of this conversation, I should be able to describe to this couple all the features they said they want in a car and all the emotions that they have surrounding the purchase and ownership of a car. I also help them identify all concerns they may have or should have if they do not make a decision now and therefore potentially lose the chance to buy the car they want. I will also help them to not get distracted by wanting a car that doesn't fulfill their list of desires, unless we discuss how they have changed their mind about the type of vehicle they want.

I might say to this couple, "So if I understand correctly, you're looking for a car that can safely carry children, can tow a small trailer or potentially a small boat, gets average gas mileage, goes quickly but doesn't have to be the fastest car on the road yet looks sharp and professional ..." I would go right down the list of all the things that are important to them. What is obvious to me, and hopefully you as well, is that they see that a fast sports car may not fit with towing a boat or providing safety for the children they want to have soon. At the end of the conversation. I would ask them if I have summarized all the things that are important to them or if I left out anything. If I left something out or misstated something, I would pause and revisit the dialogue to clear up my misunderstanding about what they were looking for in a car.

At that point, I'd be able to say one of two things: "We have a lot of cars on our lot, but there's only one or two that meet your criteria the best" or "We have a lot of cars in our lot; none of my cars meet your criteria, but I have a friend who works in another dealership, and I'd like to refer you to him to discuss that vehicle." I have walked them through a discovery process to determine what will meet their needs the best, and I have helped them to explore ideas that they may not have thought about originally.

We intentionally help patients by going through a discovery process that is well thought-out and well orchestrated.

Do you see the difference between the first sales example and the second example? The first sales process is all about me, the salesperson, making the sale that will profit me the most and selling what I assume they will like. (What professional young couple wouldn't want a fast red car?) The second example is about me being a consultant with only one agenda, which is to understand this couple so well that I am positioned to use my knowledge of cars to fit them into the most appropriate vehicle that meets their needs and desires. I am discovering everything that this couple is looking for in a car by *asking very good open-ended questions until I understand them completely*. Only at that point can I make a recommendation. Suppose the couple said, "Well, you got us right, but we're still interested in that red car over there." Certainly, a good salesperson would say, "Great. Let's talk about the red car, and let's revisit the criteria you shared with me when it comes to getting the best car for you."

I would remind them that the red car will not allow them to tow a boat and that it's not the safest car on the road when it comes to children. I will also remind them, on the positive side, that it does in fact meet some criteria in that it is fast and they will look very good in that car. Then I would ask for reclarification of which of their criteria are most important to them. This dialogue would go back and forth until eventually this young couple (the customer, client, or patient) *has a very clear understanding, perhaps for the first time*, of what they are looking for as a consumer of that product or service.

Key concept: Throughout this discovery process, I have one agenda—to find out everything about this couple, their life, how they might use the car, and what is important or not important to them when it comes to car ownership. With that information, I am in the position to act as a consultant to them and provide them with the one option (maybe two options) that will meet their desires best.

The process in scenario 2 is exactly the way that selling optimal dental care should happen. We are not trying to sell somebody something they don't want or need. That's how salespeople get a bad reputation. We are spending plenty of time with an individual (and with their significant other or supportive person), asking open-ended questions and learning about them. Those answers are sewn into a codiagnostic discovery process to determine their oral condition. From this process, you and the patient then decide what treatment best fits their desires. We are discussing optimal dentistry, so it is imperative to educate them about the actual condition of their mouth, telling them the truth, because everyone deserves to know the truth about the actual condition of their mouth. Through your simple explanation, they will know the condition of their mouth, and you will have helped them identify the pros and cons of what they're looking for. Then they will help you decide what's best for them. A wonderful book to read about selling with the customer's interests in mind is *Integrity Selling*, by Ron Willingham. Keep in mind that nothing happens until you use the skills introduced in chapter 1 to change your mindset. The above exercises are meant to provide a very logical reason why becoming the best salesperson you can be will only benefit the patient. You have to change the story you tell yourself about *your selling*. For certain, there will always be salespeople in the world who are giving a bad reputation to the word sales. That is true of any industry or profession, including dentistry. But I am not talking about the intentions of other salespeople; I am speaking to you, and when you sell your services to your patients, you are doing so because you know that when they spend their money on themselves, they are going to get more goodness and value than they paid for. The patient is the big winner when you and your team become better salespeople.

Communication

Have you noticed how often you have a conversation with someone, and they aren't even in the room? I'm not talking about texts, video conferencing, and the like. I am talking about the conversation you have in your mind with another person where you hear yourself saying something (this), and then they respond (that), then you say this, and they say that, then you say this, and they say that … we run this conversation through our head as if it is really happening. We are already predicting what the outcome will be of the conversation when it hasn't even happened yet. How could we possibly think we know exactly what the other person is going to say throughout this entire Head Trash™ conversation we have? Obviously, we cannot. We really have no idea, yet we hear the conversation in our head as if it is exactly how that conversation is going to happen. That is mindset in action, and it can tear down or build up your ability to have productive conversations.

> **The patient is the big winner when you and your team become better salespeople.**

I recently had a phone chat with Kevin, who is one of my clients. This dentist is a phenomenon. He is midway into his third decade of life, has owned a practice for less than seven years, and is collecting well over $1.5 million. I wish I had his abilities when I was his age! He wants to change his bonus system, and he has one RDH who, from his perspective, will always bring up her getting paid more money whenever he decides to make any changes in the office. This next week he is scheduled to sit down with her and have a conversation about the year that just ended, how it is great that the office revenue grew 30 percent, and the tasks he wants her to focus on this year to continue the growth.

As we chatted on the phone, he told me, "I know when I start talking to her about this past year's growth, she will say that she deserves more money because she made the growth happen."

"How do you know that?"

"Because that's what always happens when I talk to her about doing more tasks to help the office. She says if she is going to do more, she should be paid more."

There are many aspects of this employee's past behavior that contribute to my client's Head Trash™ conversation, yet you can see how real that conversation already feels to him. He hasn't even had the conversation, yet he is telling himself exactly how it is going to go, and that is exactly *how he doesn't want* the conversation to go. He can change this destructive mindset conversation by having a different conversation in his head *before* the meeting. *During* the meeting, he needs to stay focused on the outcome he desires and the assumption that he will achieve that outcome.

Therefore, before the meeting, his self-talk needs to change to, "Many of my past conversations with Debbie have ended up confrontational and left me with a bad feeling and no resolution. However,

I am now aware of how I set both of us up for a poor meeting by telling myself ahead of time what a poor meeting this will be. This time I am going to be direct with Debbie and tell her what I can and cannot do for her and tell her how much I value her as an employee. She will appreciate that. I will also tell her that even though she is not happy with my decision, my hope is that she will accept it and jump right in to help us continue to make the practice grow. I can visualize a productive conversation where I am understanding and direct with her about not getting a raise and then telling her the good news that the newly tweaked bonus system will provide her with more money."

If you don't like confrontation and you are in a conversation that feels confrontational, your default behavior (mindset) will likely be to either run away or posture aggressively. You don't physically run away; your mind runs away. That is the fight, flight, freeze, or appease reaction, and none of these reactions are helpful. In that moment, you should pause, pay attention to your emotions, and start thinking about the outcome you want. For Kevin, suppose that during the meeting, this employee is badgering him about a raise and seeming to ignore his decision not to give her a raise. In that moment, he should pause to check his emotions. If they aren't healthy, then he should direct his brain to think about the outcome he wants. For him, that is to have Debbie understand that he isn't giving her the raise she wants, but he is tweaking the bonus system so she will make more money. The very act of forcing your brain to think will reduce the emotional recoil and provide the better outcome you desire.

Improved Relationships

There are endless areas of your life where an improved mindset reflects itself in improved outcomes. I will not attempt to cover even a fraction of those aspects. However, one last area that I want to point out is your relationship with your team. You are most likely familiar with the phrase "We get more of what we pay attention to." If you want to have your dental hygienists start taking more photos of your new patients, because you're seeing lots of new patients who don't have a complete set of photos, start tracking how many complete sets of photos your hygienist is taking, and put it on a chart in your team meeting room or lunchroom so everyone can see it. Your hygienist will either start taking more photos or quit. Guaranteed.

We taught you in chapter 1 how to pay attention to your speaking negative self-talk—if you have an unsettled feeling in your gut, it is either a virus, or you are telling yourself a story that you *do not* want to come true. When you think about your team, you must start telling yourself stories that

- show your appreciation for them,

- show how proud you are of them,

- show how confident you are in their decision-making,

- show how engaged and accountable they are for their roles, and

- show what strong leaders they are becoming.

Of course, this is just the tip of the iceberg, and I hope you understand. Even if they aren't where you want them to be, notice something small but good that they do and compliment them right away. Then, when you start saying something negative to yourself about your team, stop and tell yourself a believable story that shows they are moving in the direction you want them to go.

What stories about your team have you told yourself recently that aren't the stories you want to tell? Do you hear yourself saying, "Why won't my team accept more responsibility?" or "I'm so frustrated with my team because they never …"? Ask yourself what other small but believable story could you tell yourself that is closer to the story you truly want to see happening.

Wealth

Perhaps one of the most problematic mindsets people have is around money and wealth. I would venture to say that for the vast majority of people, the word *wealth* conjures up negative images, especially in the phrase "I am wealthy." People don't seem to have any problem saying, "I am poor" or "I am broke," but I rarely hear someone say, "I am wealthy." Can you imagine going to a boat dealership, hearing a salesperson ask a potential buyer, "Would you like to buy this boat?" and hearing the response "Yes! I am wealthy," while right next to you, someone is answering the same question with "No; I'm broke, just looking."

When my wife and I were newly married, we met with a financial planner who asked me what income I wanted. At that time, I had owned my practice for two years and had just started taking home a paycheck. I responded that an income of $42,000 would be great. My wife, sitting next to me, said, "Why not an income of $88,000?" She had a much better Deserve Level™ when it came to money and income than I did.

So much negativity is associated with money and wealth. I've heard people say they are quoting the Bible with "Money is the root of all evil" or "The love of money is the root of all evil."

I love money! Early in my career, I owned an eight-year-old Subaru Outback that had 123,000 miles. I can remember one winter day driving home from my parents' house with my two kids. It was a typical cold New H winter day; the car had no heater, and I couldn't afford to get it fixed. I could see my breath in the car for most of the way home. We were not in danger of frostbite or poor health, yet it was an uncomfortable ride home. Without my knowledge, my father had put more than enough money in my toilet kit to repair the car. When I got home and discovered the money, I quickly got the car repaired.

Here is the "why" for my love of money. It is a tool. It is no different from a shovel. A shovel can be productively used to dig a hole to plant a tree or destructively used to bop someone over the head. Money is the same. It can be used to do all kinds of good things: create jobs, education, shelter, recreation, security, and so much more. Someone may look at a 240-foot superyacht and say disparaging things about the "wealthy owner." First, they don't know whether the owner donates some of the use of the yacht to help the lives of others, such as "Yachting Gives Back," where private yacht owners donate their yachts to transport food and supplies to help the homeless. Second, yacht design and fabrication provide jobs for many workers, and once afloat, the yacht provides an ongoing income for the crew and maintenance workers. I am not suggesting that you love the money itself and roll it between your fingers, though that, too, is just fine. I am suggesting that with money, you and I can do so much good in the world by deciding where it goes and whom we want to help. Focus on becoming wealthy so that you, too, can contribute in even more meaningful ways to improving the world around you.

Before you read on, stop for a moment and maybe even write in the back of this book the areas of your life where your mindset and self-talk are not aligned with what you want to happen. I just gave you food for thought by identifying mindsets in regard to business growth, sales, communications, relationships, wealth, and potential solutions.

Jot down an ever-expanding list of areas where your mindset isn't helping you achieve the goals you desire. Once you have identified these pictures and the outcome you want, you'll know the believable path of stories you can tell yourself to get those results. ⚑

KEY TAKEAWAYS

- Not only do we see the world through our subconscious, but we also see ourselves through our subconscious. This view of ourselves results in our personal Deserve Level™. We see ourselves as deserving at different levels in varied areas of our lives. While we may see ourselves deserving to play a par round of golf, we may not see ourselves deserving to have patients say yes to our treatment recommendations.
- How we see ourselves creates the outcomes we experience. When we play a par round of golf, our subconscious brain says, "That's just like you." When we begin a patient treatment presentation, our subconscious brain says, "They won't say yes to treatment because patients never accept my treatment plans." Your golf game continues at par, and your patients continue to say no to your treatment plans.

ACTION STEPS

- Write down a list of actions you could do for yourself, your family, and the world if you had more money. Post the list in a private area that you will be forced to see often, like your private home office or behind a workbench you visit frequently.
- Let that list be your armor when the jealous people of the world start telling you that you have too much money. Let the

same list be your motivation when you start hearing yourself criticizing those who have more money than you.

- Remember, once you have the money, *you* get to decide how it is spent, and you get to feel the goodness and blessings come into your life as a result of giving to yourself and the world.

PART II
LEADERSHIP

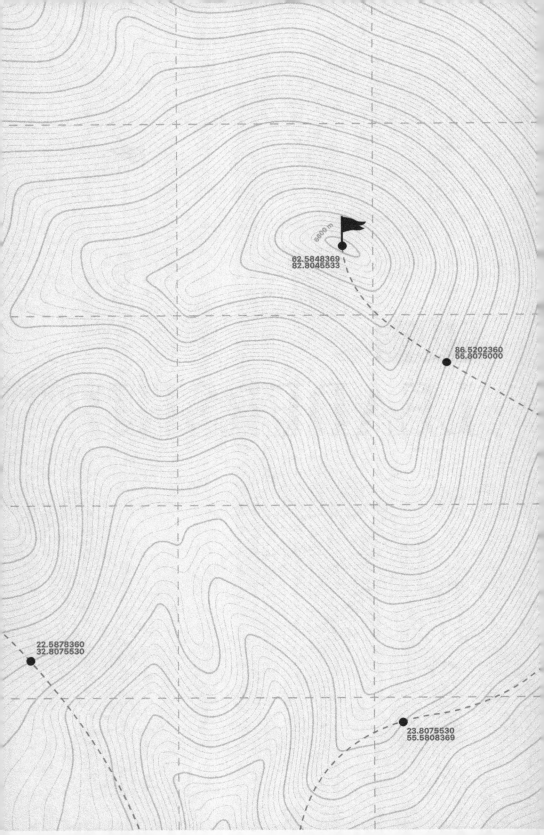

6600 m

62.5848369
82.8045533

86.5202360
55.8075000

22.5878360
32.8075530

23.8075530
55.5808369

CHAPTER 4

Leadership Is

*You cannot escape the responsibility of
tomorrow by evading it today.*

—ABRAHAM LINCOLN

Leadership is many things, and there are many things that leadership is not. When we are trying to learn what something *is*, sometimes it's easier to begin with learning what something is *not*.

Seventeen Inches

On Saturday, January 13, 1996, in Nashville, Tennessee, more than four thousand baseball coaches descended upon the Opryland Hotel for the fifty-second annual ABCA Convention. Among other speakers was Coach John Scolinos, a seventy-eight-year-old retired baseball coach whose career began in 1948. After speaking for twenty-five minutes and beginning to notice the snickering among some of the coaches, he said, "You're probably all wondering why I'm wearing home plate around my neck? I may be old, but I'm not crazy. The reason I stand before you today is to share with you baseball people what I've learned in my life, what I've learned about home plate in my seventy-eight years. Do you know how wide home plate is in Little League?" he asked the crowd.

"Seventeen inches" he heard from a few of the coaches.

"That's right," he said. "How about in Babe Ruth's day? Any Babe Ruth coaches in the house?"

"Seventeen inches?" he heard from an uncertain coach.

"That's right," said Scolinos. "How wide is home plate in high school baseball?"

"Seventeen inches," the crowd said, sounding more confident.

"You're right!" Scolinos barked. "College coaches, how wide is home plate in college?"

"Seventeen inches," the crowd said in unison.

"And you, Minor League and Major League coaches, how wide is home plate?"

"Seventeen inches!"

"*Sev-en-teen inches!*" he confirmed, his voice blasting off the walls.

"And what do they do with a Big League pitcher who can't throw the ball over the seventeen-inch plate? They send him to Pocatello!" he hollered, drawing a roar of laughter from the crowd.

"*What they don't do is say*: 'Ah, that's OK, Jimmy. If you can't hit a seventeen-inch target, we'll make it eighteen inches or nineteen inches. We'll make it twenty inches so you have a better chance of hitting it, and if you can't hit that, let us know so we can make it wider still, say, twenty-five inches.'

"Coaches, what do you do when your best player shows up late to practice? What do you do when your team rules forbid facial hair, and a guy shows up unshaven? What if he gets caught drinking? Do we hold him accountable? Or do we change the rules to fit him? Do we widen home plate?"

He turned the plate toward himself and, using a Sharpie, began to draw something. When he turned it toward the crowd, a house was revealed, complete with a freshly drawn door and two windows.

"This is the problem in our homes today. With our marriages, with the way we parent our kids. With our discipline. We don't teach accountability to our kids, and there is no consequence for failing to meet standards. We just widen the plate!

"This is the problem in our schools today. The quality of our education is going downhill fast, and teachers have been stripped of the tools they need to be successful and to educate and discipline our young people. We are allowing others to widen home plate!

"And this is the problem in the church, where powerful people in positions of authority have taken advantage of children and adults. Our church leaders are widening home plate for themselves, and we allow it.

"And the same is true with our government. Our so-called representatives make rules for us that don't apply to themselves. They take bribes from lobbyists and foreign countries. They no longer serve us. And we allow them to widen home plate!

"If I'm lucky," Coach Scolinos concluded, "you will remember one thing from this old coach today. It is this: we must always hold ourselves to a higher standard, a standard of what we know to be right. We must always hold our spouses and our children to the same standards, and we must be willing to provide a consequence when they do not meet the standard. We must be willing to hold our schools, churches, and governments to the same high standards. Be sure that you never allow yourself or others to widen the plate."

> As a leader, you know that people are depending on you and looking to you for direction.

Don't Widen the Plate

Leadership is not about accepting excuses, lowering the bar, looking the other way, or in all other ways failing to lead. As a leader, you know that people are depending on you and looking to you for direction. They need that in their lives, and you need to accept that responsibility to its fullest. Anything you don't like about your business or in your business is because of you and your lack of leadership. Anything you love about your business and are very proud of is also because of you and your ability to lead well.

Who Leads?

In any group, a leader will always emerge. Most groups have an appointed leader, either by actual appointment or by rank in the organization. However, just because someone has been appointed as the leader doesn't mean they will always be seen as the leader by the rest of the group.

Leadership is the guiding or influencing of an individual or a group of individuals. Whoever has the best capacity to do so will be seen by the group as the leader, or that individual will attempt to influence the group's thinking through their leadership qualities and behavior. What does this mean?

Unless otherwise intended, the visionary and leader should be the owner/dentist since this person has taken on all the risk and is the person who has made the fullest commitment to owning a business and delivering the products and services that they want to deliver. Over the course of the dentist's career, many team members will come and go, but the one constant is the dentist/owner who will always be there. However, there will likely be some strong personalities in the team members who will assert a leadership influence on the team and the owner. What happens when that occurs is a key element of effective leadership in the business.

Early in my career, I felt that I wanted to hire employees who were just smart enough and just motivated enough to do their job. Once employed, I wouldn't put much effort into their personal or professional development because "if they got too good, they would leave and go somewhere else." Stupid is what stupid is! It took me too long, but I learned that the best culture to embrace is one where everyone is expected to continually learn and grow and become strong leaders within their departments. As team members' leadership skills grew, they became better leaders elsewhere in their lives. They liked their personal growth, and they appreciated the opportunity that I had created where they could

> **The best culture to embrace is one where everyone is expected to continually learn and grow and become strong leaders within their departments.**

grow. Granted, sometimes it was "forced learning," yet they liked their new selves, and they were proud of themselves for having the courage to grow. And guess what? Some of them left to take on new careers, and some left for a variety of other reasons, but none left to go to another dental office. When new employees were hired into my office, the culture was in place so that if you were there, you would grow too. The veteran team members held new team members accountable, and they encouraged new team members to grow because they knew how much better their lives would be. Over the last ten years at my office, and when I sold my dental office in 2021, I received wonderful letters from the team members thanking me for giving them the opportunities to become better versions of themselves.

Leadership at All Levels

Conceptually, we can look at two different approaches to leadership. They are the Leader-Follower approach and the Leader-Leader approach. The Leader-Follower approach is structured so the leader tells the followers what to do. This limits the organization's potential since performance is totally reliant on one person's personality and competence.

The Leader-Leader model recognizes that everyone has the ability and potential to lead. It taps into individual potential at all levels, reduces dependency on a single leader, and delivers sustained performance. By adopting the Leader-Leader approach, leaders are nurtured at all levels of the organization, so there is a natural unlocking of the energy and potential of the entire organization.

Late in 1998, US Navy Commander David Marquet[6] was assigned to the USS *Santa Fe*, a nuclear submarine. The military is famous for its top-down decision-making process, so since he was both the captain and commander of his nuclear submarine, the crew expected him to make all decisions. This was the Leader-Follower approach. He wisely understood that in each of the positions on the ship, there were individuals who were in a much better position to make decisions than he was because they knew everything about that position. They may not fully understand all the elements to running the submarine and accomplishing the sub's military mission at any given point in time, but they knew their position.

What can we learn from Commander Marquet's discovery? We recommend you adopt a culture in your organization where everyone is seen and treated as leaders of their position, which is the Leader-Leader approach. To clarify, there will only be one leader of the office, and that should be you, the dentist/owner. You have developed the current vision for the business and will be the only one who can modify or adopt a new vision in the future. However, the rest of the team should become leaders in their own departments and leaders in the service side of the dental care you provide. Rather than having decisions that are made from the top down (doctor/owner decides everything and tells the team what to do), decisions are made from the bottom up.

Key concept: The Leader-Leader approach empowers. The Leader-Follower approach diminishes.

---

6   Learn more about David Marquet through his website: https://davidmarquet.com/

Leadership has nothing to do with personality. If you have been making the argument that you can never become a great leader without changing your personality, you are mistaken. History has innumerable examples of men and women who were and are amazing leaders, yet they have different personalities. Some are very charismatic and outspoken; some are quite quiet and reserved. Some make very quick decisions, and others are more deliberate in their decision-making. What you see on the outside doesn't define the great leader. However, if you could see them act, day in and day out, you would see many similarities:

- Leaders are responsible for their actions and are willing to admit their mistakes.

- Leaders express humility and gratitude regularly.

- Leaders are good communicators.

- Leaders keep their messages simple so others understand exactly what they are saying.

- Leaders have a compelling vision that is bigger than any one individual.

- Leaders are willing to make decisions and then reevaluate to make a new decision.

- Leaders accept 100 percent of the blame when something goes wrong, and they are willing to give 100 percent of the credit to their team when things go well.

- Leaders give praise quickly whenever they are aware of a team member's good decisions, actions, or excellent performance.

- Leaders encourage team members to have the courage to fail.

- Leaders encourage questions and do not strive for blind obedience.

- Leaders focus on goals and outcomes, not the methods to achieve those goals.

- Leaders use the business's noble purpose to guide all decision-making.

- Leaders recognize that new initiatives require being patient with their team and require repeating the message regularly until the action or system is being carried out with high competence.

- Leaders take care of their team so that the team knows the leader has their best interests at heart.

- Leaders constantly keep raising their expectations of themselves, their team, and their business. They see the process as a never-ending journey that supports the business's noble purpose.

That was not meant to be an exhaustive list of leader qualities, yet you can see how all of those traits can be learned. If you are naturally a celebratory person, you may readily look to catch team members in the act of doing something great and compliment them. If you are not naturally geared that way, you can train yourself to catch people in the act of doing something great and then publicly praise them. Just know that all leaders are developed and that no great leader was born that way.

Key concept: All great leaders learn to become great leaders—no one is born being a great leader.

As you look at the concept of leadership as a bottom-up decision-making process, how does that compare to what you have in your business? Do you think your team would be more engaged and accountable if they knew they would be able to contribute and make decisions? Do you get nervous thinking about giving up control and what the outcome might be if you were not "in charge"? Take a moment to jot down the scenarios where you feel it would be beneficial to give your team leadership responsibilities in their department. ⚑

KEY TAKEAWAYS

- Leadership is a mindset issue, and anyone can improve their leadership capabilities because great leaders learn to become great leaders; they aren't born that way.
- There are essentially two models of leadership—leadership from the top down or leadership from the bottom up. The Leader-Follower model implies an autocratic culture where the leader/dentist makes all the decisions and hands out the rules while the team dutifully carry out their wishes. The Leader-Leader model implies that the team members at all levels want to perform better in their departments and have their ideas listened to and implemented as to how the business operates. To have an engaged team who wants to expand the business's noble purpose, the Leader-Leader model is the best and perhaps only effective model.

ACTION STEPS

- This week, identify one situation where you routinely "widen the plate" for one of your employees by not holding them accountable to perform a task to expected performance level.

- Look at your employees and see if any have never done a particular task well. If so, then at the very least, they may need better training, so you should train them. If their quality is sometimes very good at a particular task, but it is inconsistent, immediately have an individual meeting and point out the inconsistency since there may be an attitude issue playing out, not a skill-level issue.

- Ask your team to explain to you and each other how team consistency will give all patients the same excellent service. Then let them know they have to choose between consistently great effort and outcomes or finding another employer who will "widen the plate."

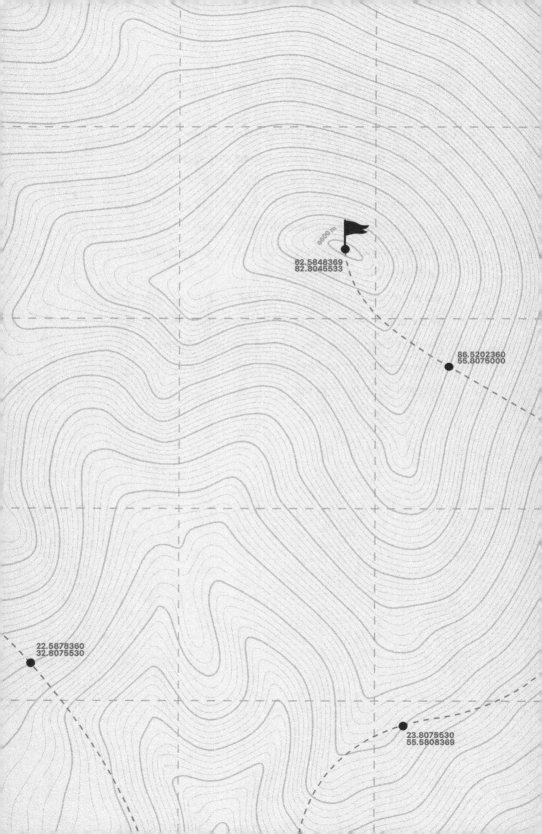

CHAPTER 5

Leadership in Action

The way to get started is to quit talking and begin doing.

—WALT DISNEY

Early in my career, I can recall going to a number of two-to-three-day practice management seminars and the team coming away with a really great feeling. Then on Monday morning, I realized that I didn't really have any concrete ideas that I could put into place. The weekend course had provided lots of great concepts that filled me with hope, yet come Monday morning, I had no tangible action plan to achieve the results discussed at the course. I wrote this chapter in such a way that on Monday morning, you can open it up and make actionable leadership changes.

Vision

At the top of the leader's responsibility is setting a crystal-clear vision or noble purpose for the business. The noble purpose can be developed with or without the team, but it is the owner who needs to fully embrace this purpose. For instance, if you are starting a new dental office and you don't have a team yet, your initial marketing and thought processes must revolve around the business's noble purpose. When you have a team and you have not yet identified a vision or noble purpose for the business, then involve the team in the process. Schedule a half-day meeting with the conversation directed toward answering each of these two questions:

- What do we look like when we are at our best?
- What do we want to look like when we are at our best?

These two questions will allow you to focus your thoughts and conversations to develop a clearer picture of who you already are or who you want to become.

As an example, my office employees and I saw the impact we were having on patients who accepted optimal full-mouth dentistry. This was especially true for the patients who had lost their ability to eat the foods they wanted, live without dental pain, and smile without consciously covering their mouths or turning away. When optimal dental care changed their mouths and smiles, they changed. These patients became outwardly joyful and happy, smiling more often and taking more pride in their outward appearance. Their spouses made comments like "My husband/wife is more fun to live with because of the work you did." What we knew was that we were on track and fulfilling our noble purpose: "Improving people's lives, one smile at a time."

I discovered I had personal airway issues that impacted my ability to wake up refreshed. Long story short, I got treated for sleep-disordered breathing, and that journey had a positive effect on my life. And in the same vein, our office's noble purpose was to "Improve people's lives," and creating better sleep certainly put joy in my heart and a smile on my face. Incorporating dental sleep medicine into the business fit the business's noble purpose, so that became a new service and journey for my team and me.

Once you have your noble purpose in writing, you must remind your team of that commitment on a consistent basis. This may seem unnecessary, but I assure you that in the hustle of your day-to-day business, it is easy for the team and you to become distracted and stop doing all the little steps that move you toward your vision.

> **Once you have your Noble Purpose in writing, you must remind your team of that commitment on a consistent basis.**

Core Beliefs

With a guiding star in your noble purpose, you need to determine who you are and who your team members are at the core of their being. We all have our core beliefs and core values, so they aren't something you think up. They are already in you, and they simply need to be identified and written down.

An easy thirty-minute exercise is to ask each of your team to write down the names of three famous people they admire and three family members or friends they admire. Next to each of these names, they write down what characteristics they see in that person that they admire. Over the following twenty minutes, you will identify five to seven common theme values that everything gets distilled into.

For instance, your team comes up with the following list of traits:

- Constantly gets better

- Believes in education

- Wrote a book

- Is smart

You work together, and you decide that you distill and condense these similar ideas into the term "lifelong learners." One of your written core values is "We are lifelong learners."

Organizational Chart

Every major corporation has an organized chart that identifies the necessary positions in the company, the top three to five roles of that position, and the name of the person assigned to each position. This chart has different names, such as *organizational chart, organizational board, accountability chart*, and *institutional structure*, to name a few. You can search online for various examples of what an organizational chart (OC) can look like. The size and number of your OC will depend on the size of your business. For instance, the typical dental office has four to fourteen employees, so those companies will likely need the following positions:

- Visionary: The owner/doctor at the top of the OC.

- COO/Integrator/OM: In charge of all operations, right under the visionary.

- Clinical: In charge of all clinical matters, right under the COO.

- Business operations: All financial, insurance and money issues, right under the COO.

- General operations: IT and all maintenance, right under the COO.

- Marketing: In charge of all internal and external marketing, right under the COO.

- Under clinical are dentist, hygienist, and dental assistants.

- Under business operations are finances, treatment coordinator, bookkeeping, and concierge.

- Under marketing are internal and external.

- Under general operations are IT/equipment and building maintenance.

In a much bigger organization, other positions are needed like CFO, CEO, and CIO. Many more positions get added in bigger companies, but for the typical dental office with revenue of less than $5 million and three or fewer locations, the OC I just laid out will suffice.

Once you and your team have laid out the OC with all the positions, you need to assign the most vital three to five roles of each position. Once you have done that, you need to assign one person to each position. This is a critical step. For a smaller company like the average dental office, it is likely that the same person will be in multiple positions. That is fine. However, for each position, you and your team must do the following:

- Ask for a volunteer for each position.

- Once you have a volunteer, ask the volunteer if they want to be in charge of that position, whether they understand what is required of the position, and whether they accept the responsibility of the position.

- Assuming they say yes to all the above, then each team member and the doctors must verbally agree the person in that position is able to do the job. If anyone objects, then you have to discuss that to determine why they object and decide whether to change the name or accept that someone objects to that person being in that position.

- If no one volunteers for a position, you'll need to hire someone to fill that position. It is likely that someone on your team will volunteer for all positions, except possibly the COO position. The person in this position has to have the ability to remind team members and doctors of their role responsibilities. Sometimes this is an unpopular task, so the best personality for this position is someone who isn't concerned when another team member is upset with them. They are just doing their job.

Let's summarize what you just created and how powerful these three steps are.

1. The noble purpose gives you direction, and anytime you are unsure about a decision or the actions of a team member, you can ask yourself and the team, "When we do _____, are we at our best?" Or asked another way, "Does what happened yesterday represent us at our best?" Assuming you have a strong team that agrees with and wants to support your noble purpose, they will see their error and have the desire to do better next time. We learn from our mistakes.

2. Core values are much the same as the noble purpose, though at a different level. For example, you decide to have the whole team start reading books together that will add to their personal development. Someone on the team is resistant, citing that they would have to do it at home, and they don't get paid for that. You remind them of three of your core values:

   ▸ We are lifelong learners.

   ▸ We are hard workers.

   ▸ We do what is right, regardless of the inconvenience to ourselves.

3. Then we ask team members to help you understand how their seeming resistance to book reading fits with the core values they agreed to uphold. This tool helps you and the team members decide whether they are a good fit for this business. If not, you help them find a different business that has different core values or is willing to look the other way. (Remember what Coach Scolinos said about widening the plate.)

4. The organizational chart assigns every task and duty in the office to one individual. When something is done well and done right, the team member in charge can hold their head high. When something isn't done or done well, it is clear who is in charge, and the situation is addressed to the person in charge. Without making one person in charge, many things don't get done, and the response is "It isn't my job" or "I thought _____ was going to do that."

With these three actions in place and the whole team agreeing on them, you have created a structure where everyone knows who is responsible for what, and everyone's actions can be measured against an agreed-upon noble purpose for the business and individual core beliefs as to how they will behave. Of course, this does not create perfection. Humans will make mistakes, unintentionally and intentionally. However, with this structure, a team member who doesn't fit in anymore or shouldn't have been hired in the first place will stick out like a sore thumb. On the other hand, the awesome and amazing team members will love this structure since they will know exactly what is expected of them, and they will know when they are performing well.

As the leader of your business, by putting in these three actions, you have stepped up to the plate and created the infrastructure of accountability to roles, positions, and the culture (values) of the office. Now let's look at what it looks like to push leadership down into your organization.

Leader-Leader

A key concept in the Leader-Leader style of leadership we discussed in chapter 3 is that the dentist is the primary leader and responsible for the operations of the entire business as well as the outcomes that result from the actions of the entire team. An example of the Leader-Leader style of leadership is found in the chronicles of Commander David Marquet, who was the captain of the *Santa Fe* nuclear submarine in the late 1900s.

For Commander David Marquet, much is at stake when you have nuclear warheads on your ship, where the proper outcome is to make the right decision about whether to launch a nuclear missile. Naturally, with so much at stake, the military thought it best to put Captain Marquet in charge of making every decision, no matter how small. How small is small? When Captain Marquet first took command of his submarine, he was in charge of approving or declining a day off from work that one of his 135 crew members asked for. Therefore, initially, he had to review the HR booklet to find out the guidelines and look into the on-duty record for each specific sailor. Then he would have to decide to approve or disapprove the time-off request, provide the fourteen steps of written documentation, and notify the seaman of the decision. All this, while running a nuclear submarine!

This may seem crazy, yet you'll likely find some areas in your own business where you still hold the reins on making decisions in areas where someone else on your team is more qualified. For some decisions, you don't know enough to make the best decision (e.g., the best source to buy XYZ bonding agent). For other decisions, another team member has much more knowledge than you about what goes into making the best decision (e.g., an insurance claim has been returned with the request for a second narrative).

Commander Marquet realized that there were many highly trained and capable individuals on his ship. Given their skill, they should be either making all the decisions in their department, or they should be analyzing the issue and then arriving at the potential solutions. With the Leader-Leader model, the seamen were empowered to use their knowledge and experience to identify the real issue, come up with what they felt was the best solution, then present that solution to their immediate supervisor. That process resulted in what is called an *"I intend to"* statement.

> **Key concept:** The team is responsible for arriving at what they feel is the best solution to an issue, then presenting that solution to their manager, the integrator, or the dentist/owner.

So in your business, whenever a decision needs to be made, the team member who is accountable for that position has a responsibility to think through the issue and consider the possible solutions. Then they decide the best solution, come to their manager, and say, "Here is an issue or opportunity, and having thought it through, *I intend to* …" On the flip side, whenever a team member tries to avoid being a leader and comes to the dentist asking what the dentist wants them to do, the dentist supports this team member's leadership growth by not answering that question, rather responding with: "I want to support your growth as a leader, so kindly tell me the potential solutions and what you intend to do."

Since infancy, we have been told what to do. As young children, what we learned was that if we did what we were told to do, we made our parents and teachers happy, and they rewarded us. What did the rewards look like? They often sounded like:

- "Good job, Johnny. I love it when you pick up your toys when you're asked."

- "Class, I want you all to be like Suzy and put away your books when I ask."

We learn at a very young age that there are societal rules that tell us how to act and what to think and that if we follow those rules, we are rewarded. Getting rewarded feels good. We also learn that when we do not follow the rules, we are punished, and punishment doesn't feel good. So what do we all do? We follow the rules, and when in doubt, we ask someone how they want us to do it. This is pounded into every one of us, so we all develop many of the same default behaviors when it comes to deciding on our own. When faced with a decision, we tend to gravitate toward "Just tell me what to do." It takes away any accountability we have for the outcome.

If you tell someone what to do and it doesn't work out, they feel it isn't their fault because *you told them* what to do. The *I intend to* statement is created when an employee has thought through the issue and solutions, but they haven't acted yet. The team member approaches the dentist/owner to make sure what they intend to do is the best solution, and then the best action can be taken.

I have talked at length about the Leader-Leader versus Leader-Follower models of leadership. We simply want to impress on the owner/leader that your job is always to support your team. That support needs to be in all areas of their personal and professional growth. You must not contribute to the Leader-Follower model by not being patient with the team's growth into their leadership position. Most notably, when a team member comes to the owner/dentist and asks, "How do you want me to do this?" the owner/dentist may be very used to giving the team member the answer. However, by doing so, you are undermining your team member's growth into the "I intend to" level of leadership. The supportive dentist's response should be: "I want to fully support you in your leadership growth, Mary, so what are the possible answers to the question you just posed to me?" The dentist/leader should help the team member identify their possible solutions, provide the dentist's solutions, and then determine which solution is best. At that point, the dentist can compliment the team member and say: "That's perfect, Mary. You came up with some very good solutions, and you were able to identify which of the solutions seemed best to you. In the future, I would like you to keep stepping into your leadership role by performing that same process on your own and then coming to me with the 'I intend to' conversation we described. Be patient with yourself, Mary, as this will take time until it becomes a natural process for you. I will do my best to support you in your growth by not giving you an answer until you have thought through the possible solutions and recommended to me which you feel is best."

The team member will feel supported by the leader when the leader takes the time to show the team member what the process looks like and tells the employee what the leader expects in the future. Some team members will learn this quicker than others, so you need to be patient with each individual and let them grow at their own pace. Let progress and not perfection be your guide.

With these systems in place, you have laid the foundation for accountability and team member ownership of their roles in the office. Let's look at some of the specific actions and characteristics that are common among successful leaders that you can begin to incorporate into your daily life to become a more impactful leader:

- Right people on the bus
- Communication
- Integrity/transparency
- Authenticity
- Open-mindedness
- Emotional intelligence
- Decision-making
- Vulnerability
- Delegation
- Tough love

Right People on the Bus

In his best-selling book *Good to Great*, Jim Collins correctly identified the need for every business to have employees who understand and embrace the business's vision or noble purpose.[7] We identified the leader's responsibility to create a crystal-clear vision or noble purpose in the last chapter. When you are hiring or evaluating an existing team member, their alignment with your company's noble purpose is crucial. The right team members will embrace your noble purpose and feel energized working in your business. Their individual life purpose will resonate with the business's noble purpose. This cohesion between the individual's and business's noble purpose results in a team member who willingly works hard to make sure that the business does well. These team members still want other benefits, yet they will feel an alignment with the business and that alone will make them feel good. Anyone who loses interest in the business's noble purpose or demonstrates a greater desire to put their personal interests above those of the business is not a good fit. Collins would say they are not the right person to be on this bus, because this bus is going someplace (vision or noble purpose) that this employee doesn't want to go. Everyone is better served by either not hiring this individual or helping this employee find a new place to work that more closely aligns with their personal life vision. You, the leader, must identify these situations. Before you hire someone, be certain they embrace your company's noble purpose as well as your company's core values. Don't hire someone who doesn't fit with your noble purpose, and terminate an employee who no longer supports the vision or core values.

---

7   Jim Collins, *Good to Great*. London: Random House Business Books, 2001.

Communication

We humans communicate all day through our words and actions. Certainly, we have all heard the phrase "Your actions speak so loudly that I cannot hear what you are saying," or "Actions speak louder than words." A leader must verbally and nonverbally communicate the vision and do so frequently. What does this look like? I tell you to put every team member in charge of tracking certain metrics and statistics for themselves and the business. With all that focus on numbers and money, it can be easy to forget why you are there. It is the leader's responsibility to verbally remind the team that despite our focus on numbers, the numbers are just a measurement of how well we are succeeding in our purpose.

As an example, suppose there are two different dental practices in the same town, and both perform optimal dental care. They have the same fees and team size and work the same number of days each year. One office collects $2 million a year, while the other office collects $1 million. Since they are doing the same optimal care, then the $2 million office is helping twice as many people as the $1 million office.

The leader needs to constantly remind the team that increasing revenue is simply a metric of how successfully they are at getting patients to say *yes* to optimal care. The more patients they help say *yes*, the more revenue the business collects. The focus is on helping patients, and the outcome of that focus is that the business has greater revenue.

Additionally, the leader must look for teaching moments when team members are acting in ways that don't align with the business's noble purpose. These moments are simply reminders, and they can sound something like this: "Yesterday, I overheard Mary [RDH] and John [TC] speaking with raised voices and harsh tones. Since I heard it in my treatment room, our patients also heard the conversation. Is that who we are when we are at our best?"

It is the leader's responsibility to make sure this topic is brought up and brought up in a way that allows the team to be reminded and to grow. This is not meant to be punitive in any way. It provides an opportunity to pause and see how we can change the way we act in the future so that we are focusing on giving our patients our very best. The conversation should address what the conversation was about. For example: How do we communicate without raising voices (attacking), and how, when, and where do we have these inevitable conversations between team members? It's OK to disagree, but it is not OK to be disagreeable. Effective leaders get these issues into the open and don't let them fester or allow issues to be left unaddressed.

Integrity/Transparency

A respected leader commits to telling the truth and simultaneously showing complete respect to the individuals they are speaking to. Telling the truth seems easy, yet it can be difficult and deceptive. Consider whether the team needs to know everything that is on the owner's/dentist's mind? I will unequivocally say no. For instance, say the office cash flow is low, and at the same time, a very large onetime expense is due. You are nervous about being able to pay all the bills for the next couple of months. Should the team be told that it will be hard for the business to afford payroll? The thought process of a business owner or entrepreneur and that of an employee are very different. A business owner and leader knows that from month to month, year to year, there will be ups and downs. Many employees live in the moment. In the last example, their minds may hear "I'm not going to get paid" or "This business is failing, and I need to find another job."

The owner or leader sharing their nervousness only creates chaos and distracts the team from focusing on great patient care.

When the leader decides that something needs to be addressed, then that communication needs to be direct—no sugarcoating—in such a way that the message and its delivery show complete truthfulness and respect for the individual or group.

Authenticity

Great leaders come in all different shapes and sizes. You may have a big personality or be quiet and reserved. Nothing about your personality determines whether you become an effective leader. Therefore, be yourself. Do not try to emulate the way another person leads, though you can learn from their methods. What does that look like? Regardless of how you present yourself, you need to keep reminding your team of the vision and what that looks like in your day-to-day office flow. This reminder should be done face to face, not in a text or email. Therefore, find a time when a brief conversation can occur with added clarity as needed. This needs to be done in such a way that the team members all feel respected. Yet how the message is delivered should be the real you, speaking as you are the most comfortable.

Open-Mindedness

As the business leader, you want to foster the Leader-Leader model, and therefore you must be open to your team's ideas. Most people are used to being told what to do, and for them to step out of their comfort zone and offer a new idea requires the leader to be very willing to engage in listening to others' ideas. Here are a few helpful methods to create open dialogue:

- Never use the word "but." Substitute the word "and" whenever you would ordinarily use the word "but."

- Never ask a question by beginning with the word "why." Instead, ask the same question, but start the sentence with the word "what" or "how."

For example, suppose a team member suggests a marketing idea that you tried three times in the past, and it always failed. If you are the team member, how do you feel when your boss says: "I like your idea of the billboard, Mary, *but* ..." (See how, as soon as you say, "but," she is expecting rejection of her idea?)

Now consider this response: "I like your idea of the billboard, Mary, *and* ..." This way, you can introduce your thoughts to the mix of ideas, and Mary is still feeling that her idea is respected. It doesn't mean you will use her idea; it simply means you will entertain her idea with more conversation, and Mary feels heard and respected. This will encourage her leadership and her motivation to offer more suggestions and ideas in the future.

Key concept: Use the word *and*, not *but*.

Resist the temptation to use the word "why" to start a question. When you begin a question with the word "why," you make the other person feel defensive. By asking why someone does something, they must justify themselves to you or justify their actions to you. When you substitute the word "how or "what" for the word "why," you are asking to learn from that person. Asking to learn makes them the expert who is telling you the reason behind what they do.

Rather than saying, "Why do you take a full set of photos for each NP?" ask, "How does taking a full set of photos for every NP help your NP process?" or "What part of your NP process benefits when you take a full set of photos?"

Key concept: Never use the word *why*. Instead, substitute the words *how* or *what*.

Additionally, as you keep the conversation active and alive, with everyone having their opportunity to share their opinions, there is a much greater likelihood that the team will come up with the best idea. The more ideas, the better chance that together you will come up with the best solution. Also, when the team comes up with an idea that gets implemented, they instinctively work harder to make it work, simply because it was their idea, and they want their idea to work well.

Emotional Intelligence

Emotional intelligence (otherwise known as emotional quotient or EQ) is the ability to understand, use, and manage your own emotions in positive ways to relieve stress, communicate effectively, empathize with others, overcome challenges, and defuse conflict. To put this into action, anytime you are in a conversation with another individual, keep in mind your desired outcome. How is that helpful? You will certainly find yourself engaged in important conversations that feel confrontational. You may be tempted to go to your default, which may be to verbally put someone down or try to convince others of your point of view. In these situations, you'll likely need to check yourself and see whether you are trying to win the conversation or what your emotional agenda is. Often, you'll find that you're feeling conflict, so you are reacting in a foolish manner by reacting in one of these four incorrect ways:

- **Flight.** Emotionally run away and disengage from the conversation.

- **Fight.** Raise your voice or lean into someone.

- **Freeze.** You shut down and lose your train of thought (freeze).

- **Appease.** You don't want to be confrontational, so you give in to something you don't believe in just to keep the peace.

Those four reactions—fight, flight, freeze, or appease—are very common reactions, but they are all the wrong reactions since none of these will result in the outcome you desire. Instead, pause, take a slow breath, focus on the outcome you want, and then proceed.

Decision-Making

There is a fun phrase that says, "You cannot steer a parked car." Essentially, this phrase means you've got to be moving to change direction. Some leaders struggle with making decisions for fear of making the wrong decision. With very few exceptions, all decisions can be revisited, so in the future, a new decision can be made. The greatest leaders will tell you that they made lots of poor decisions, but they were open to the idea that the decisions they made could be constantly reevaluated. If a decision doesn't work out as well as you wished, go back to your team or coaches, look at the facts, and feel free to make a new decision.

We are not advocating that your decision-making be erratic without any obvious process or basis. What we are saying is not to get caught in the trap of feeling like you have to have all possible facts before deciding. Oftentimes, those who wait will miss out on a golden opportunity.

How decisions are made in your organization should be clarified for the team at the beginning of all conversations since there are four decision-making methods:

1. Autocratic

2. Consultative

3. Majority prevails

4. Consensus

Let's define each of these four different methods of decision-making in the dentist-office setting:

Autocratic. The dentist will make the decision, and they don't need to or intend to consult with the team.

Consultative. The dentist will make the decision, and they want to thoroughly understand the ideas and thoughts of the entire team on this matter. Once the dentist has heard each of the team members, and each of the team members feels the dentist has heard and understands their ideas and feelings, then the dentist makes the final decision.

Majority prevails. Everyone shares their ideas and opinions, and regardless of who has what opinion, the choice that receives the agreed-upon percentage of votes will be the accepted decision. If there are multiple options to vote on or an odd number of team members, including the doctors, then the owner/dentist will cast the tie-breaking vote.

Consensus. Everyone shares their ideas and opinions, and there is no decision until everyone agrees, including the doctor/owner.

At the beginning of any discussion or meeting where decisions will be made, the leader needs to be verbally clear to all team members as to how the decision will be made. For example, if the team thinks they will decide by everyone agreeing (consensus), and you, the owner, want to hear the team's ideas, and then you will make the decision on your own (consultative), some team members may be very upset to hear your decision when they don't agree with it (if a 100 percent consensus was never reached). Most autocratic decisions are purely owner issues that don't affect the team, so they occur infrequently. For example, there is an opportunity to refinance the office debt that will improve the financial responsibility for the owner. It doesn't affect the team members, but it is a decision that the business must make, so the owner makes it on their own without team input.

Likewise, relatively few decisions will be made by consensus, as getting everyone to agree on one decision can be torturous. These issues are usually decisions for which the owner/dentist isn't concerned about the outcome since all possible outcomes are fine. An example may be the choice of restaurant for the annual Christmas dinner celebration.

All team members should be reminded, including the owner/ dentist, that for all decisions (except autocratic decisions), each team member will have a chance to air their thoughts, and all opinions will be respectfully considered. However, once everyone has been heard and a decision is made, whether you agree or disagree with the decision, everyone must embrace the decision as if it were their idea. To do anything less than support all the office's decisions is being a poor team member and likely conflicts with your written core values.

You must make sure that whoever is running a meeting has a high emotional intelligence and is a good communicator. Meetings are needed to bring up issues (positive and negative), gather solutions, and make decisions, yet they have the potential to be complaining sessions and time wasters. The dentist/leader must continually develop communication skills to keep meetings and conversations on target, so the intended outcome is achieved.

Vulnerability

Different cultures feel differently about showing emotion in a business climate. For many individuals, especially men, being vulnerable is seen as a weakness. For those who feel that way, consider the following scenario.

Suppose you are in an audience of five hundred people, and the speaker is sharing something emotional and intimate to them, and many in the crowd are tearful as they listen to the speaker share their moving story. If you were in the crowd, and the person sitting next to you said, "Wow, I would never have the courage to stand up there and share that personal story," would you say, "Yeah, neither would I," or would you say, "Oh, that guy on stage is weak; that's why he stood up in front of five hundred people and told his very personal and emotional story"?

Being vulnerable takes courage simply because publicly exposing what you see as a personal weakness means taking a risk of being hurt. People will not physically hurt you, but they can emotionally hurt you by verbally dismissing your feelings as being stupid or wrong.

As a strong leader, you want your team to grow, and therefore they will make mistakes. We learn best from our mistakes, and sometimes the individual team member's mistakes will be known to all. They may feel vulnerable when their mistakes are known. A leader will encourage a team culture where, whenever something goes wrong, everyone accepts responsibility for their part in the error. For those who have a hard time admitting when they have failed, this admission can make them feel very vulnerable. The wise leader will share some areas of their own that make them emotional and vulnerable. This demonstration by the leader is just another example of the leader showing what they want from their team by sharing their own words and actions.

Delegation

Part of leadership is delegation, and the best leaders will delegate often. Wise leaders delegate tasks and decisions at many different levels. From a team member's perspective, if the dentist/leader only delegates the menial and boring tasks to them, they don't feel valued, and their leadership isn't enhanced. However, when a team member sees that a duty has been delegated to them that has great importance, they will feel a sense of honor for having been trusted with this duty. Prior to delegating a challenging duty to a team member, be sure to consider the two rules of delegation: the team member needs to have (1) competence and (2) clarity around the duty they are being asked to do. This does not mean that they have done the task before but that they are skilled enough, and with appropriate guidance, they will succeed. I suggest that when a team member has 80 percent competence in an area, they are ready to assume more duties in that area while continuing to gain excellence and mastery in the current duties.

A team member needs to have complete clarity on what the required outcome is and why that outcome is required. That clarity allows them to understand the importance of the assignment they have been chosen for.

Tough Love

It's lonely at the top. Being the leader of a business requires making decisions that are not going to please everyone. In those moments, there may be some team members who are not rallying around the decision because it wasn't their idea, or they feel the wrong decision was made. The decision-making process must be done so that every team member's opinion is openly heard and "put on the table" for all to consider. When that is done and a decision is made, all team members must accept that decision and support it. They must act as if the decision were their idea. Sometimes, a team member may continue to argue against a decision or, after the meeting, make comments about how they feel the decision is a poor one. At moments like this, the leader must accept their responsibility to go to this team member and have a sincere conversation about the agreements the team has made, the values they all hold dear, and the business's noble purpose.

As a reference, a good parent, when faced with being a parent or being their child's friend, must always choose to be the parent. This needs to be done with love and respect, but the effective parent doesn't stop being a parent when they think their child might not "like them" in that moment. Likewise, as the leader of your business, you'll need to accept the fact that when needed, you'll have to put your "friendship" with a team member aside and let them know that how they are behaving is unacceptable.

As you do more and more optimal dental care, we will suggest that you'll have some of these "tough love" conversations with your patients. Optimal dentistry requires having a relationship with your patient. It isn't like the relationship you have with your family or spouse, but it will be a significant relationship. Consider the following scenario:

Your spouse comes home from a doctor's appointment and tells you they have cancer. You ask them what they are going to do, and they tell you, "Nothing," and then they walk away. Is that likely the end of the conversation? Do you accept that and let them do nothing? No! Why not? Because you love them, and you care for them too much to let them just do nothing.

As we stated, your relationships with your patients are not like the one you share with your spouse, but ask yourself this question: Why do we give up so quickly on our patients the first time they say no to our recommended treatment?

Understand this: they are saying no to themselves, not to the treatment you are recommending. We always suggest you push past the first "no" because you care enough for this person that you want to explore with them why they are not getting done what you know will help them in so many ways.

Key concept: Care enough about your relationship with your patients to *help them get past their initial "no" responses to optimal care.*

I shared a list of some of the common skills seen in successful leaders earlier in the chapter. Reflect on the list and honestly evaluate your leadership skills. In the book's margin, rate yourself from 1 to 10 next to each skill. Identify the skill you rated lowest and decide on one small action you will do for the next twenty-eight days. Commit to that, then come back to your list and pick the second lowest area. You'll see yourself improving, you'll feel the power you're creating inside you, and your team will respond to your improved leadership. ⚑

KEY TAKEAWAYS

- Incredible business success is dependent on providing a layered structure for the right people to work within. That structure involves identifying and writing down the business's noble purpose and core values. These two entities serve as the barometer to gauge employee issues.
- The third layer is creating an organizational chart that identifies who does what. With these three layers in place, you can quickly identify issues in your office as either people issues or training issues. Imagine how easy life will be as the dentist/leader when all your frustrations are neatly placed into one of two boxes.
- If someone we love is ignoring a significant medical condition, we feel our duty is to determine what's preventing them from seeking treatment. Sometimes, we are outright forceful as we challenge them about accepting their poor health. If we truly care about the welfare of our patients, we should stay engaged in our conversations with them, even when they say no or suggest they are not going to get healthy.
- Treat your patients more like you do those you dearly love. Show them you care enough about them that you stay engaged to help them get out of their own way and become healthy by accepting your treatment.

ACTION STEPS

- In order to get the desired response from conversations, replace the word *why* with the words *how* or *what*. The word "why" forces the listener to defend their position. Rather than make the listener feel defensive, reword your phrase, and by using *how* or *what*, you are asking the listener to teach you how their idea works. Everyone likes to be the authority and tell you how to do something, so they change from being defensive to being eager to share their ideas with you.

- At all your future team meetings, let your team know at the beginning of the meeting or with each new topic how the decision will be made. If you want their input, and then you will decide, verbally let everyone know. If you will only accept a decision that everyone agrees on, let everyone know, and be prepared to have multiple meetings until a unanimous decision is made. If you would like the decision to be unanimous, but you have to decide by the end of the meeting, then announce that you would like a unanimous decision, and you will decide with their input if the team cannot totally agree by the end of this meeting.

PART III
OPERATIONS

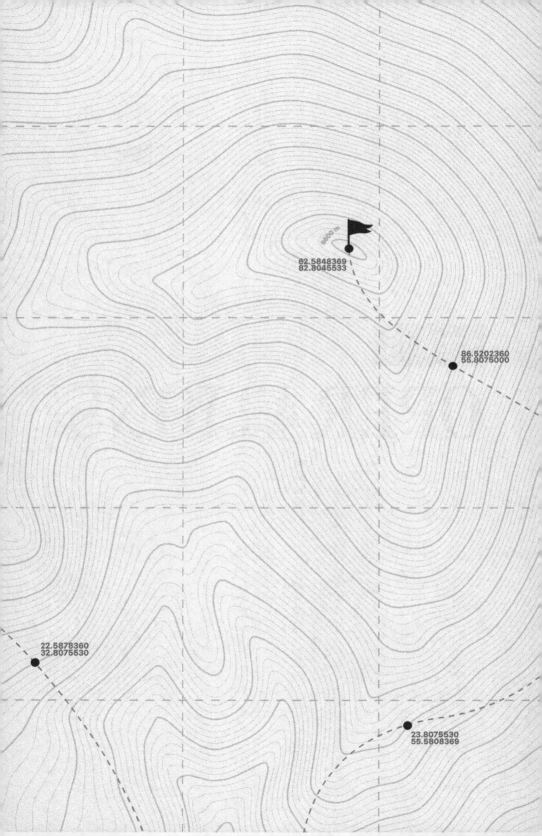

62.5848369
82.8045533

86.5202360
55.8075000

22.5878360
32.8075530

23.8075530
55.5808369

CHAPTER 6

Effective Administration

If it's not written down, it does not exist.

—PHILIPPE KRUTCHEN

You now embrace the power behind thinking well and telling yourself a better story, and you have committed to improved leader skills. As a great thinking leader, you still need to create highly organized processes to achieve team engagement and deliver optimal patient experiences.

On the surface, McDonald's and your dental practice have nothing in common, though they should. The quality of their food is poor. Occasionally, they have good hospitality. They *always* have the same end product. If you eat at McDonald's, then you know you can go to any of their stores in any country, and your favorite food will look and taste the same. In 1948, Maurice and Richard McDonald decided to sell hamburgers and shakes in their San Bernadino drive-through restaurant. Modeling their restaurant after the automobile assembly lines in Detroit, they birthed the fast-food industry by premaking their burgers and keeping them warm under heat lamps. Today, McDonald's is completely systems driven. That is their genius and the explanation for why you get the same food item, no matter which McDonald's you frequent. Additionally, you have to wonder how they can routinely replace employees, yet their product output is still consistent. This chapter will be very mechanical because that is where the rubber meets the road. You want your business to be organized and spin like a top, which frees up your team to spend time giving patients an amazing relationship experience, not wasting time due to disorganized or inefficient systems.

Write It Down

Your office needs to have a written systems manual, and the systems need to be clear, simplified, and current. Every process in your office that has an outcome needs to have a written system to support the flow of information, materials, and effort such that a brand-new employee can create virtually the same outcome as a seasoned employee. Imagine how freeing your office will be when a new employee can go to a system manual and learn how to do any process in your office. I am not suggesting that this manual will allow a new team member to be just as efficient and create the same relationship experience as a highly skilled veteran employee. However, the manual allows a new employee to understand the process leading up to every outcome and *why* the system is important. Every system in your manual needs to start out with *why* that system is important to your office's operation, and most likely, it will always be tied back to how it supports your business's noble purpose or your core values.

I will provide you with an example of a system we used in my office for calling patients either before or after a procedure and calling to thank new patient referrals. All systems must answer the following questions:

- Why?

- Who?

- How?

- When?

- What notes?

System name: Nonscheduling Patient Calls

Why: We are an empathetic, relationship-focused team, and our patients deserve to know we want the best for them, even when they are not in the office.

Who:

- RDH to SRP/STMP patient on the night of treatment.

- RDH to NP two days in advance to introduce themselves and see if NP has questions.

- Doctor to post op. all surgery, sedation, and long Tx visits (1.5+ hours)

- Doctor to patient who refers another patient: "Thank you for referring [NP's name]."

Process:

- CDA: Each day, red Sharpie, paper schedule, circle patient's names, Dr. P. to call.

- CDA: Beginning of appt, verify patient's current best phone number and update patient's chart as needed. Put number on schedule PRN.

- CDA: Hand Dr. P. marked schedule at p.m. huddle.

- Dr. P.: Call patients at night, leave message if no answer. Send text only if cannot leave a voice mail (e.g., mailbox full, not set up).

Scripts

- Dr. to treatment patient when leaving a message: "Hi, this is Dr. Pearce calling to speak with [patient's first name]. I just wanted to touch base with you after today's visit to make sure you are doing well and see if you have questions. No news is good news, so I will assume you are doing well, but that said, if you are inclined to call the office tomorrow and let us know how you are doing, that would be great. I want to congratulate you on a job well done today. I don't take it for granted that what you had done today is easy. You did wonderfully. I am proud of you and your commitment to have wonderful dental health [or a gorgeous smile]. Have a great evening, [patient's first name]. Goodbye."

- Dr. to referring patient: "Hi, this is Dr. Pearce. I want to thank you for referring [NP's full name] to our office. I feel great earning your trust, and I will make sure we do the same for [NP's first name]. If you feel I should know anything about [NP's first name], feel free to call me at this number, which is my cell phone. Otherwise, thank you again, and have a great evening."

- RDH to NP: Call two to three days in advance. *This is not a reminder for the upcoming visit*, so make no mention of that. The purpose of the call is to begin to establish a close relationship and make our office and RDH stand out compared to the average office. You'll likely leave a message, so it can sound like this: "Hi. My name is [clinician's first name], and I am calling from Dr. Pearce's office. I will be seeing you, [patient's first name], this [*day only* of their appointment], and I wanted to reach out to you in advance to welcome you to the office and tell you that I am excited to meet you. I also wondered what I can do now to make your [day of the week] visit easier. Feel free to return my call for anything you feel will be helpful for me to know. Otherwise, I look forward to seeing you, [patient's first name]. Have a wonderful day. Goodbye."

- Use the patient's first name at least twice in the message. Everyone likes to be identified by their own name. This is the start to establishing the personal nature of your relationship with this person.

Chart Notes

- RDH and Dr. P.: Use Autonote to record conversation to chart.

- Dr. P: Autonote. Dr. P.—Postprocedure call by doctor to patient. Left message re: call office if any concerns.

- RDH: Autonote. RDH: Called NP. No answer, so left message per NP per appointment call script.

- Note: The NP that the RDH is calling may not have a chart to record notes in, so the day of the NP visit in the a.m. huddle, the RDH discusses the call that occurred with the NP team when discussing the opportunities for today's patients.

As you can see, the system must be detailed, step by step, and it must be thorough. Your system for the same process will have the same steps; only the *how* will differ.

Now that you know why you need systems, and now that I have given you an example of how you should lay out the structure of each system, let's look at some of the more important systems you should have.

Sales Process

In chapter 3, we discussed the mindset around selling, and I hope you embraced that and are willing to be very intentional about helping patients say yes to your optimal dental care. I like to visualize the sales process like an Olympic relay race. In this race, the success of the next runner is initially determined completely by the proper handoff from the runner before them. One bobbled handoff, and the team will not win the race. Likewise, in your sales process, everyone has their role in the process, and the better they do their job and hand off their piece to the next team member, the more likely you will win, and the patient will say yes to your recommended treatment. The sequence of events is this:

- Proper website and marketing attract patients who want what you offer.

- NP call specialist does all NP calls and is skilled in making amazing calls, with relationship-building notes taken from each call.

- Concierge welcome by Patient Coordinator to NP when they arrive to your office.

- First Triangle of Trust handoff from Tx Coordinator to RDH in consult room.

- RDH creates relationship and NP codiscovery using photos and active listening.

- Second Triangle of Trust from RDH to doctor in treatment room.

- Third Triangle of Trust from RDH to Tx Coordinator in consult room.

- Schedule and follow-up protocols followed.

All system outcomes are determined by the weakest link, so each individual needs to be at their best with the patient and with their handoff to the next team member.

New Patient (NP) Call

An excellent new patient call requires good active listening and outcome-driven communication skills. Our profession has trained patients to think insurance is important, so NPs often begin the call by asking insurance questions. Your office is familiar with NPs asking, "Do you accept my insurance?" NPs are calling your dental office to get help with a dental issue, not to take an office survey to see which offices accept which insurance. I am not saying that insurance isn't important to them. I am saying they want to find a dentist they can trust who can help them, not write a report about what offices accept which insurance. Therefore, your treatment coordinator must be skilled in minimizing time spent discussing insurance and maximizing time spent developing the relationship. This involves finding out what is important to the NP and determining why your office is a good fit for the NP. All humans have an emotional reason for the actions they take, so this call needs to be focused on what is the driving emotional force behind this NP deciding to pick up the phone *today* to call you. They could have called you last week or put it off another week, yet they called you *today*. Your NP specialist must develop the skills to ask better open-ended questions so that you know what the NP's motivating emotion is.

Triangle of Trust (TOT)

Have you ever experienced a dental patient who says they want all the treatment you presented to them in your treatment room? You're feeling good about the conversation when you take them to the financial person/scheduler. You tell your scheduling/financial teammate what the patient needs, or you say, "The next step is in the chart." You finish that quick exchange, turn to the patient, and say, "So nice to meet you today, Sally, and I look forward to seeing you at your next visit." At the end of the day, you find out *they scheduled nothing!* Most of my new clients say it happens all day long.

What occurred is you were not able to get a complete yes to treatment in the clinical setting, and the financial person didn't have the knowledge or the relationship to provide the missing information or handle the patient's objections. The end result is that the patient leaves your office without scheduling, and you didn't accomplish your noble purpose to help them say yes. Just as in a relay race, a bobbled handoff of the baton results in a lost race—the poor or missing transfer of information from one team member to the next in the patient's presence will no doubt end up in a "no." However, when this is done properly, the transfer of information sets the next team member up for success, and the patient gets the treatment they want and deserve. We refer to this process as the Triangle of Trust, and it should happen every time a patient is being passed from one clinician to another.

Key concept: The Triangle of Trust sets the next team member up for their success.

New Patient: TC to Clinician Triangle of Trust

The TC is involved in the triangle of trust when the next step is for a patient to make a payment and/or schedule treatment. The NP initial phone call will usually be handled by the Treatment Coordinator (TC) since that is their designated action. The fully trained TC will follow the guidelines for the NP call, as I just discussed.

The NP arrives, and after the PC provides the concierge/hospitality welcome, the first triangle of trust occurs when the NP, the TC, and the RDH all meet in a conference room. Two days before, the RDH called this NP and left a hello message, as laid out in the system example earlier in this chapter, so the clinician and the NP have spoken but have never met each other.

The TC introduces the NP to the RDH and briefly reviews the information from the NP call that she recorded on NP's Telephone Call Intake Form. All of us have experienced poor customer service, where you tell your story to one employee of a company who passes you to the next person, who has none of your information, so you repeat everything. That is unacceptably poor service for you and your team. You are striving to provide top-shelf customer service.

The TC's introduction of the patient to the clinician may sound like this: "Mary [the RDH], I'd like you to meet Joe [the NP]. Joe and I spoke last week, and Joe has had a very difficult time with dentistry in the past [you're beginning to hear Joe's emotional position on dentistry]. He feels like his past dentist didn't listen to him and that the hygienist was rough. When he asked questions, he felt like they didn't care about him, and he felt like he was just a number."

TC looks at Joe and asks, "Joe, am I on track so far?" Joe will clarify as needed. TC continues.

"Joe shared that he has heard there are solutions for his poor smile. He was at a sales meeting recently, and a customer commented on his poor smile, which was embarrassing. Joe also shared that he feels his smile has been interfering with his social life, and he wants to do something about it. He heard about our office on the radio, and he got the courage to call us. [Turns to look at Joe.] I am so glad you did, Joe. You are in the right place. Joe, did I get everything right, or did I leave out anything you want Mary and me to know?" Joe responds to clarify or say it all sounds accurate.

TC says, "Joe, I know you will have an amazing visit today with Mary, and I look forward to seeing you after your visit when you can share with me your amazing plan to get the smile you deserve."

TC leaves the consult room. At Mary's discretion, she and Joe may stay for a while longer if Mary feels she needs more information about Joe's concerns. When Mary feels she knows all she needs to know for now, she escorts Joe to her treatment room.

NP: RDH to TC Triangle of Trust (TOT)

After the RDH completes the NP visit with the NP, the next TOT, which involves the treatment coordinator, will occur. The only exception to this is when the NP only needs a re-care appointment, with no other recommended treatment. *Otherwise, the TOT should always happen.*

Key concept: Whenever you notice your treatment acceptance percentage is falling, examine the occurrence and effectiveness of your TOTs as a likely source of the problem.

Five minutes prior to the clinician bringing a patient to the consultation area, the clinician notifies the TC using the intraoffice headset system. The TC goes into the consult room and pulls up the NP's full face/full smile image on the computer. Now the NP's pictures are visible as they enter the consultation room. This TOT is led by the RDH, whereas the first TOT was led by the treatment coordinator.

TC to Clinician Follow-Up Visit

The more optimal treatment you diagnose and recommend, the more instances you will have when patients need longer to process the information fully before they will commit to treatment. Understand that a patient who doesn't say yes is not a patient who is saying no.

Key concept: A patient who is not saying yes to treatment is not a patient who is saying no to treatment.

How is this so? Consider that before they say yes to your treatment recommendations, they will need to process the following:

- They may need more time to process what they heard.

- They may need to speak with the dentist again to confirm their gut feeling that they trust this dentist to do their treatment.

- They may need more information, etc.

- They may need to bring their spouse into the office to gain their support (though you should always have their spouse or significant other present when presenting optimal treatment).

- They may need to figure out the financial commitment prior to signing the financial agreement.

Keep moving patients along the sales process while having patience with their decision-making progress. When a patient returns to the office to discuss their dental care a second or third time, the TC and clinician will enter into another TOT. The patient is seated in the consultation room, the TC does a brief interview to see what questions or concerns the patient has, then uses the office communication system to let the doctor know they are ready. This TOT may sound like this:

"Dr. _____, Joe and I have been talking about his poor smile. Joe shared with me that he feels he cannot afford to do the full treatment you discussed last time and would like to revisit the options you discussed. Joe really likes the plan he chose last time, but after thinking about it, he wants to look at other options. Did I get that right, Joe?"

The dentist will then handle the rest of the visit with the TC actively listening for any areas that need further clarification. For instance, the TC may notice that when the doctor mentioned the treatment would start with the lower back teeth, the patient seemed to frown at that, but the doctor kept going. So, the TC may say something like, "Joe, a couple of minutes ago, Dr. _____ mentioned that the treatment would begin on the lower back teeth, and I sense you had a question about that. How do you feel about starting there?"

Most of the conversation is led by the dentist, and the TC has a significant responsibility to look for body language, tone, silence, or other cues signaling that the patient is not fully on board with what the dentist is saying. Usually, patients do not want a lesser treatment plan, even though they appear to be asking for that. They simply need reassurance that they are making a wise decision and the value from the dental care will be far greater than the investment they make. All TOTs should have pretreatment full face/full smile pictures on the consultation room computer or TV screen. As the old adage goes, "A picture is worth a thousand words." The patient has gotten "used to" the look of their smile as it gradually deteriorated over the years. Putting it up on the screen simply shows the truthful condition of their mouth. It serves to remind the patient of the emotional reasons they came for help in the first place.

Meetings

Meetings are critical for you and your team to be on the same page and to get everyone's ideas so the very best decisions can be made. I will highlight the basics of which meetings are critical and why, though the scope of this book doesn't allow for complete dissection of all meeting systems.

> **Key concept:** The problem with communication is that we think it occurred.

I will continually emphasize that you and your team are at your best when everyone is present, so everyone needs to be present and on time for all meetings.

Different meetings have different purposes, and they should be structured as such. I recommend you have five different types of meetings that are held regularly and are structured. All meetings, except the quarterly and annual meetings, should be held in the office.

- **Daily huddles.** An a.m. huddle at the beginning of the day and a p.m. huddle at the end of the day.

- **Weekly team meeting.** Ninety minutes per week, same day, same time for the whole team to discuss last week's team and individual metrics and make decisions on issues.

- **Individual meetings**

  ‣ **New hire.** First few weeks after a new employee begins.

  ‣ **Weekly team member meetings.** Twenty minutes one day each week. The doctor and a team member meet each week to discuss their lives inside and outside the office. Creates employer/employee appreciation.

  ‣ **Annual team member meetings.** Review of each team member's growth for the past year. Opportunity to define new individual growth goals and how the office can support the team member as they pursue that growth.

- **Learning meeting.** Two to four hours per cycle (twelve/year) to advance team learning.

- **Quarterly and annual meetings.** Off-site full day of planning to revisit the last ninety days, set new ninety-day and twelve-month goals, and revisit your three-year and ten-year business goals.

Daily Team Huddles

The operations concept for morning and evening meetings is to look for opportunities on that day to help patients say yes to treatment recommendations, to ask for referrals, to collect owed money, and to arrange prepayments for future treatment. Each day we are focused on today, so we only discuss today, not yesterday or tomorrow.

A.M. Huddle

This meeting occurs during the first fifteen minutes of the day. Each clinician (RDH and CDA) arrives prepared to verbally tell the team the total outstanding proposed dentistry they have for the patients scheduled in their chair and identify at least one patient that they will focus on who has the greatest opportunity or who is most likely to move forward with treatment.

The treatment coordinator verbally lists the six to ten patients who will be contacted today to follow up on proposed treatment. The patient coordinator identifies the total outstanding accounts receivable dollars that will be collected from today's patients.

Even if goals are not met and opportunities are not captured, the tone and spirit of the meeting is that "we did our best, we learned what we can, and tomorrow is a new day with fresh opportunity."

P.M. Huddle

This ten-minute meeting occurs at the end of the day. The PC announces the total production and revenue for the day, progress on this cycle's goal, and their success collecting past-due AR. The TC reports the follow-up call successes. Each team member announces their individual success for the opportunities they identified at the a.m. huddle, plus any other opportunities new to the schedule since the a.m. huddle. Each team member verbally states what follow-up can be done for all patients they saw today who did not accept treatment. The doctor is actively listening and coaching as able while looking for team member successes that can be acknowledged and celebrated. Of course, there are always opportunities for celebrations every day, and it is the doctor's responsibility to look for those and let them rise to the surface. Even if goals are not met and opportunities are not captured, the tone and spirit of the meeting is that "we did our best, we learned what we can, and tomorrow is a new day with fresh opportunity."

Weekly Business Meeting

This ninety-minute meeting is scheduled at the same time every week with the same format. Here are the guidelines for a successful weekly team meeting.

RULES

- Everyone shows up five minutes early so the meeting starts on time. We have to respect ourselves, our teammates, and the noble purpose of our business.

- Everyone participates.

- Always start on time and finish on time. Use a timer on someone's phone or stopwatch.

- Integrator runs the meeting. You can substitute another individual, but they must be able to confidently keep the meeting on track and quiet side conversations. Doctor never runs the meeting.

- Everyone comes prepared with the metrics they are responsible for.

FORMAT (AGENDA)

- Segue: Everyone gets settled in and chitchat out of the way (five minutes).

- Scorecard: Compare to last week. Make an issue of thirteen-week trends not on target (five minutes).

- Rock review: All individuals/company. If not on track, make it an issue (five minutes).

- Customer/team headlines: Patients/team news (five minutes).

- To-do list: Go over last meeting's to-do list. If not done, becomes an issue (five minutes).

- Issues: Identify, discuss, and solve all issues. Discuss revenue/prod first (sixty minutes).

- Conclude: Recap new to-do list. Rate the meeting 1 to 10 by all team members/doctor (five minutes).

The "scorecard" is a sheet for the business and individuals that allows for the important measurables to be tracked week by week. The team is responsible for collecting the data and entering it. This scorecard will give you a quick pulse of how the business and individuals are doing and will give you an accurate picture of the patterns and trends for the five to fifteen most important metrics in your business.

Sample scorecard layout:

OWNER METRIC GOAL							
Current Week*	6/12	6/5	5/29	5/15	5/8	5/1
Jenna P. Avg. Accd. Tx.	$2,000	$3,516	$1,262	$2,006	$8,126	$286
Chris R. % Pts. Rescd.	95%	94%	97%	89%	94%	93%
*6/13 weeks shown						

Ninety-day tasks are the building blocks that work toward the one-year goal. In actuality, you start with a three-year goal. Then decide where your business must be in one year, to be on track for the three-year goal. Then you decide where you need to be in ninety days so that you are on the right trajectory to reach your one-year goal. Every team member has a company ninety-day goal and a ninety-day personal growth goal. Each individual quickly reports that they are either on target to meet their ninety-day goals or not.

Issues are simply any topic that needs discussion. The initial focus of the meeting is to discuss any revenue or production targets for the last week that were missed and identify where they occurred and what can be done differently to get back on track for next week. Three issues are identified at a time, and once those three are decided on, then three more issues are chosen. The meeting is run by the same person each week, and that person is charged to keep the meeting on track, prevent sidebar conversations, and stick to the agenda.

A to-do list is generated, which assigns tasks to one individual, and these tasks are simplified so they can be accomplished by next week's ninety-minute business meeting.

The conclusion is a verbal summary of the to-dos that have been made.

Lastly, everyone scores the effectiveness of the meeting from 1 to 10. The parameters of a successful meeting are as follows:

- Everyone participated.

- Issues were thoroughly fleshed out, and everyone felt their ideas were heard and considered.

- The meeting was kept on track, and no one monopolized the conversation.

- There was no politicking—trying to convince others that one's position on a subject is correct.

- Decisions were made.

- The meeting had energy, and all team members were engaged.

Individual Daily/Weekly Meetings

NEW HIRE

Newly hired team members are always under stress as they try to figure out how to fit in with the new office. Of course, they want to succeed, and they want to avoid failure. The dentist/leader needs to meet with the newly hired team members daily for the first few weeks to touch base and get a gut feeling of how they are doing with the stress of the new position. The leader needs to be encouraging and look for ways that the new hire is succeeding while encouraging the new hire to be patient with themselves. These "touching base" meetings continue for as long as the leader feels they are needed, until the new hire begins to feel accepted and friendships are developing between the new hire and other teammates. Ask your team how the new hire is making out, since they can see the new hire's progress and they want this person to succeed as much as you do.

WEEKLY INDIVIDUAL MEETINGS

All team members want to feel appreciated by the dentist/leader, and a great way to foster that is to connect with each team member to discuss how their life is going, both inside and outside the office. Schedule a twenty-minute brown-bag lunch on the same day each week. Meet with a different team member each week to discuss whatever they want to talk about, with the focus on their family life, not their office life. Take these meetings very seriously since, once you start offering this opportunity to connect with your team, they will want to continue, and some will truly look forward to uninterrupted one-on-one time with you.

ANNUAL INDIVIDUAL MEETINGS

Part of the leader's responsibility is to ensure that team members have an opportunity to continually grow, both professionally and personally. Setting annual individual goals is integral for employees to feel the sense of accomplishment and mastery of their jobs. Mastery doesn't mean they are awesome at every aspect of their job. Mastery applies to specific areas of their overall role. By continually challenging employees to grow personally and professionally, you are setting them up to feel engaged in their current jobs and also creating skills and attributes that may allow them to move their career in other directions. Nothing can be more gratifying to an employee and the leader than to have established such a strong culture of learning and growth in your business that team members move on to even more challenging careers. Only goodness comes from establishing this growth culture.

Schedule an initial brown-bag lunch timed around the employee's annual anniversary. You may need more than one brown-bag lunch to reach the final plan, so do not expect that one brown-bag lunch will be enough time to lay out the next twelve months for every employee. The team member needs to bring evidence to the meeting that they have put effort into the last twelve months' goals and show where they have progressed. All annual goals must be easily measurable so the employee can quantify what they have accomplished. Also, a measurable goal prevents the employee from hiding behind fluffy progress statements that sound nice but do not translate into any actual progress. Here's an example. A fluffy goal is: "I will improve my leadership skills." A clearer and better goal is: "I will identify and read four books on leadership and then write five skills from each book that I will put into action in my day-to-day work."

> **Only goodness comes from establishing this growth culture.**

LEARNING MEETINGS

These two-to-four-hour meetings are held monthly once on the same day of the month.

These meetings are to advance team and doctor learning, not to discuss business issues. It may be used to discuss interpersonal team issues as that is often an area that can create team growth and intimacy. All teams experience times when interpersonal tension strains team harmony. This meeting allows for "the elephant in the room" to be exposed and discussed. This process may not be "fun," but it does allow for the team to be vulnerable around each other, and inevitably this will lead to individual growth and a stronger, more engaged team.

Other planned forms of learning that are scheduled in this meeting are:

- **WIL.** The What I Learned (WIL) is the first activity of this meeting. Each team member identifies one small learning tied to their primary role and therefore advances the company's noble purpose. Each team member also verbally announces their last six cycles' WILs and how they have continued to incorporate those actions. This review serves as a reminder for all of their prior commitments to learning. If the employee hasn't continued to use the learning from the past, this serves as a reminder to them, not a punishment. We all need reminding of what we know we should do and have let slide out of our focus.

- **Books.** All team members read the same book and discuss what they learned from the book. Each team member also tells what they reported learning from the books read at each of the last six monthly learning meetings. This review is meant to create forced learning since it forces team members to repeat what they say they "learned" over the last six months. True learning means changing how we think or act, so this exercise puts pressure on "the thinking or acting differently" aspect of learning.

- **In-house training.** Hiring leadership coaches to come to the office and conduct leadership exercises.

- **Recordings.** Listening to brief (ten-to-fifteen-minute) CDs on some aspect of leadership, sales, or mindset development and then exploring how to use that information as a growth challenge.

- **Role-playing.** Model different pushback scenarios that team members actually experienced the past week when speaking with patients about treatment. Also model using open-ended questions and active listening skills to delve deeper into the emotional reasons why patients say yes or no to our treatment recommendations.

Quarterly and Annual Meetings

These off-site meetings are a full day when you and your team examine your progress and connect as a team. The agenda and facilitation can be done by the dentist/leader, or a facilitator can be hired to organize and run the meeting. All the basic business tenets are reexamined to see if any changes should be made to the organizational chart or individual roles within that chart. In no particular order, the following basic business aspects are examined and changed as needed:

- Marketing strategy.

- Accountability chart.

- Values.

- Organizational checkup.

- Team members: Any new members that need to be brought up to speed.

- Team engagement: Any perceived issues.

- Business profitability.

- Ninety-day goals: Individual and team—review last ninety-day goals; develop and assign new individual ninety-day goals and new team/business ninety-day goals.

- One-year plan.

- Three-year picture.

In addition to the above, the annual meeting will also review the prior year, asking these four questions:

- What did we do well?

- What did not go well?

- Where are opportunities to further our purpose?

- What decisions can we make?

These scheduled meetings are designed to accomplish different objectives. That said, the office culture needs to be one of "*we are a dental family,* and we need to take care of each other." Therefore, there will be unscheduled meetings between the doctor and team members (and between team members) when interpersonal issues arise that need to be shared or resolved.

As you read through the system examples, are you able to identify areas in your office where your systems may need some attention? A wonderful idea I learned from a colleague is to have your team create or update one system each month. Once they do this, the revised system is circulated for all team members to comment on or sign off on. With five or six team members, you'll be updating sixty to seventy systems each year, which will keep your system manual complete and current. ⚑

KEY TAKEAWAYS

- Your business needs to have written systems so that you can expect the same outcome for every task, every time it is done, no matter which team member does it. The systems are not designed to create robots out of humans, yet they provide enough guidance and clarity to allow different individuals to arrive at the same outcome. Not only do systems provide consistent outcomes, but they also free up employee thinking so they can focus on more important tasks, like communicating with patients about the amazing opportunity to become dentally healthy.

- Predictable meetings are critical for high-rpm teams to have effective communication and collaboration. A short morning and end-of-day "huddle" allows for successful identification and follow-up on patient treatment opportunities. A highly structured weekly business meeting allows for the continuous flow of ideas, discussions, decisions, and assignments to individual team members, while a longer monthly learning meeting supports a lifelong learning office culture and provides a forum for professional and personal growth.

ACTION STEPS

- The lifeblood of all dental offices is new patients, so make your first and best system your NP call. Create an NP call form that requires the team member speaking to an NP to follow a system to get the desired result. I feel that NP calls must create a significant relationship with the caller, and therefore, the beginning of the call is focused on learning why the NP called *today*. The skilled team member will learn to discover the emotion behind why the person is calling the dentist and, in particular, your office. Conversations about money and insurance need to be skillfully handled so the patient gets off the phone feeling they had a wonderful call with an empathetic and kind person who works in an amazing dental office. Train your team to orchestrate this call, and put the systems in place for that training to occur and be reinforced.

- Begin having weekly ninety-minute business meetings, occurring at the same time, on the same day, and with the same format. A team member should facilitate the meeting so that digression off-topic isn't allowed. The process and outcome are that all team members enter issues they want to discuss, the team decides each set of three topics to be discussed, everyone is required to provide input, decisions are made, and a to-do list is divided up and assigned to individuals.

- Each week, the prior week's to-do list is revisited to be sure each team member has completed the assignment they said they would do. The outcome of this meeting is whole-team involvement with decision-making on relevant issues, and one individual is held responsible for each task. With one person in charge, the tasks get done with no one saying, "I thought _____ was going to do that."

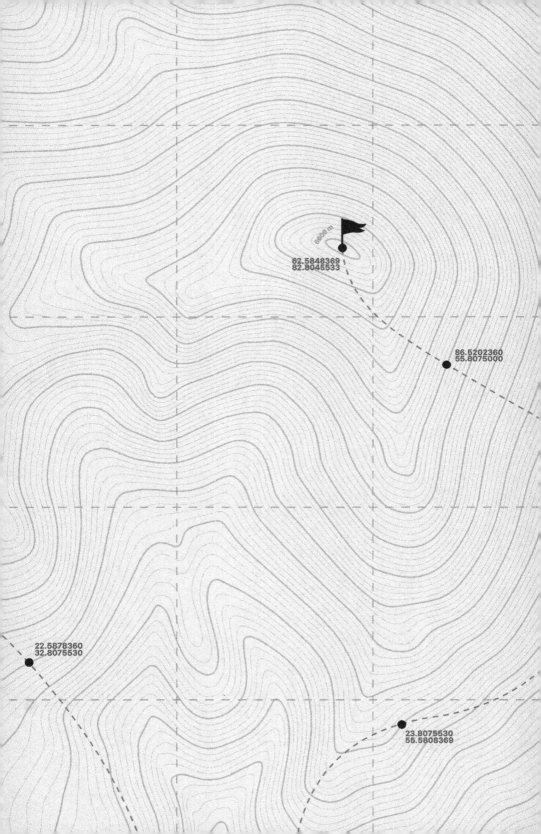

CHAPTER 7

Clinical Systems

A good system shortens the road to the goal.

—ORISON SWETT MARDEN

In *The Checklist Manifesto: How to Get Things Right*,[8] author Atul Gawande identified that with the explosion of science and technology, the challenge has moved from being ignorant to being inept. Checklists provide a mental safety net against predictable human lapses in memory, focus, and attention to detail, and Gawande found many industries that have been using them for years.

When I went through dental school, composite filling materials were just coming out, while silver amalgam was still the preferred

---

8   Atul Gawande, *The Checklist Manifesto: How to Get Things Right* (London: Picador, 2011).

filling material. Once the tooth was prepared, a ZOE base might be applied, then cavity varnish, and finally the silver amalgam. Three steps. Today, composite fillings are placed more often than silver amalgam, and the composite filling requires many more steps.

This book will not be able to address all the clinical systems that your office should have, yet we will help you decide where you need them and their key attributes.

Checklists

A good checklist will be precise, efficient, practical, and easy to use even in the most difficult situation. Don't try to spell out every detail. A good checklist will provide reminders of only the most important steps that even a veteran employee could miss.

> **Each procedure should have a separate checklist listing all items required for that procedure.**

For each checklist, place a "pause point," which is when the checklist should be used and decide whether you want a do-confirm checklist or a read-do checklist. With the former, you set up everything you think you need, then you look at the checklist to verify that everything is done. With the latter, you read each step and complete it before moving onto the next item on the checklist.

Each procedure should have a separate checklist listing all items required for that procedure. For a new hire, that may mean they have everything in plain view before the patient is seated (read-do). A veteran CDA may only set up the basics for a certain procedure, since they know they will have time to finish the rest of the setup while the patient is being anesthetized. That said, all aspects of the room setup that require moving equipment or placing items in the patient's direct view should always be *done before seating the patient*. Items in direct patient view should be covered in some manner (plastic/metal cassette cover, patient bib, sterile wrap, etc.) so the patient isn't forced to watch you set up the room in front of them. The materials/instruments setup behind the patient's head can be done after seating the patient. Patients don't want to see you setting up the instruments that will be used for their procedure since those instruments can be associated with unpleasant thoughts in their minds.

Checklists can be computer generated for each of today's patients, or you can have a laminated printout with a dry-erase marker to check off each item. Don't micromanage this process. However, if every week you have a CDA getting up to get something on the checklist, then go back to pulling the checklist in a read-do fashion. The same standards apply to RDHs. The captain of every airline flight has the same checklist for every flight they fly, and they are meticulous in ensuring that every item is checked because your flying safety, and theirs, is at stake. In your office, your reputation and efficiency are at stake, so hold yourselves to high standards. As a reference, a highly skilled and organized CDA should rarely (less than once per month) leave the treatment room, even though they are setting up for complex surgical procedures.

Headsets

Headsets are now everyday items in virtually all businesses. If you are not yet using them, you and your team will love them when you try them. Two-way radios offer dental offices a better way to effectively communicate between team members without disrupting the relaxed environment you offer your patients. These radios and earpieces improve teamwork, reducing stress by communicating in real time without wondering whether someone got your message. There are many manufacturers, though Motorola has a good reputation in this space.

All team members except the doctor wear their headsets and wear them all day. The PC has a separate phone headset used to answer the phone from anywhere in the office when they are not at their desk.

While using these radios, keep conversations to a minimum with no chitchat regarding nonurgent matters. For example, a conversation about what someone wants for lunch today is not a headset topic, as it creates a distraction for the entire team. Monitor yourselves, and don't allow frivolous chat over the radios. Chitchat conversations are great; just have them without using the radios.

For maximum efficiency, ask for the receiving team member's attention before speaking. For instance, when a CDA wants to let the PC know they are bringing a patient to the front, the CDA would say, "Mary [the PC], can you hear me?" The CDA *will not continue* until Mary acknowledges her. Mary is obligated to respond, just like in a face-to-face verbal conversation when you need to know the receiver heard your message. We *don't want* the CDA to simply say, "Mary, I am bringing [her current patient's name] up to you now," and then bring the patient up front. Until Mary responds, the CDA doesn't know:

- if Mary is at her desk,

- if Mary heard her say she is bringing the patient upfront, or

- if Mary wants the CDA to bring the patient up front right now.

Supplies (Clinical Only)

There are so many clinical supplies today that a well-designed and easily monitored system is vital. This system will require more effort to set up than any other system, and it can easily fall apart if the system isn't completely laid out. Remember that all systems are outcome driven, so initially determine the outcome you need for each step in your system.

Keep the supply system for clinical and administrative (nonclinical) separate from each other. For the clinical supplies, put a clinical team member in charge. This system can be laid out on paper, on the office software, or an Excel spreadsheet. The vehicle to maintain the supplies doesn't matter as long as the components are obvious and accountable. Below I have laid out the system we used in my office, which worked very well. You can duplicate ours or create your own. If you create your own, you'll want the following features:

- Central inventory location

- All supplies centrally located if possible

If you don't have enough open space to put all clinical supplies in one location, then have one central supply area used as your primary inventory. When needed, move supplies from the central location to designated areas closer to the treatment rooms. Those locations may be the sterilization area, lab, or the treatment room drawers.

The central inventory area should be created with the following thoughts in mind:

- Have a barcoded system or tag system so reordering is timely and accurate.

- Make an arrangement with one dental supply company to maintain your supplies. Use the same company to service your dental equipment and purchase new office equipment.

- Put one person in charge of ordering supplies.

- Have a follow-up system that makes sure the entire order has been placed and received.

- Back-ordered items are accounted for and a determination is made if another supplier should be contacted. You need to know if another supplier was contacted so supplies aren't completely depleted.

- The role of opening shipments is assigned to one individual.

- Develop a process to add new products to central storage with simultaneous update of the barcode or tag system.

Central Clinical Inventory Area

Ideally, you'll keep all clinical supplies in the same area, yet many offices do not have enough space to place all items in one location. Either way, be sure that all supplies used in different departments are arranged together. Additionally, make sure there is a separate section for shared products. For example, all these products should be stored together in the storage area:

- Hygiene: Includes any item specific to hygiene alone.

- Restorative: Separate the different items used in each restorative procedure, and keep all those supplies in the same location.

- Composite materials: Matrices, wedges, bonding agents, etc.

- Prosthetics: PVS impressions, impression trays, scanning disposables.

- Surgery: Membranes, screws, bone, phlebotomy supplies, etc.

- Orthodontic: Fixed or clear aligners.

- Dental sleep medicine: Sleep-protocol-dependent supplies.

- Whitening: Even if done by a RDH, technically it is not a hygiene-only procedure.

- Endodontics.

- Pedodontics.

- IV sedation.

- Oral medicine: Store separately if you feel it cannot be included with surgery.

Be sure to allow empty space in each area so that when restocking items, there is plenty of available space to restock where the items belong. Never put the same items in different locations, unless one is the central inventory and the second is a much smaller staging area used to move products into the treatment rooms as needed.

Key concept: Never store the same item in different inventory locations. This leads to outdated items, excess inventory, and wasted time spent determining the actual inventory of any product.

If you cannot put all the above products in one central inventory area, then put all of each category in one spot. For instance, if there isn't enough room for everything in the central storage area, then all the surgical supplies could go in designated cabinets in the lab. If you use this method, put barcodes/tags on these storage area shelves in the other area that is not the central inventory area.

Barcoding or Labeling Tags

The central inventory area and staging area shelves need a barcode or a description (tag system) for each product. This barcode or description is attached to the front of the shelf with the reorder guidelines:

- Quantity remaining on the shelf left when it is time to order

- Number of units to reorder

For example, the 2% Lidocaine with 1/100 epi tag might look like this: "2% Lidocaine, 1/100 epi 2/5." This means that when there are only *two boxes* of Lidocaine with 1:100 epinephrine left on the shelf, *five boxes* need to be ordered.

You decide how many of each item needs to be reordered at any given time, but the general idea is that if something doesn't have a shelf life, have at least one month's supply on hand. You should never run out of any supply, yet you do not want months' or years' supplies of some items in the office. Having an excess of product and supplies is disadvantageous because:

1. you want to control the expenses paid out of the office, and

2. you want to remain flexible. If you want to substitute one product for another, you don't have to throw out unused products or spend years using up a product before switching to the new product.

At a glance, this system allows anyone to determine how many units are left on the shelf, when it is time to reorder, and how many units should be reordered. For certain products, it is acceptable to wait until you take the last of that product off the shelf before reordering, though you must make sure the item taken will last a long time before it needs reordering.

For example, in my office, a box of Geistlich 40x50 mm Bio-Gide membranes would last three months. We knew we could get a new box in a couple weeks, so the reorder tag reads: "Geistlich 40 x 50mm Bio-Gide 0/1." This means: wait until you take the last box off the shelf (0) and then order one (1) new box.

If a barcode system is impractical for reordering, or your supply representative is resistant to setting up the system for you, then place a descriptive tag with the product and reordering instructions. This system requires more work, as the items to be reordered must be written down, rather than experiencing the convenience of scanning with a barcode scanner.

Ordering

Time is money. I liked creating the opportunity for our dental-supply representative to place all our product orders and run our ordering and restocking program for us. These salespeople receive a commission on volume, and at the very least, their company wants more of your business. Do not waste a team member's time shopping around for the

> **Do not waste a team member's time shopping around for the best deal on products. The cost savings doesn't outweigh the poor use of the team member's time.**

best deal on products. The cost savings doesn't outweigh the poor use of the team member's time. Streamline or outsource as many of the redundant tasks as you can. Ordering supplies does not add to their personal or professional development. If your current supply representative resists setting up and maintaining your inventory system, speak with the supply company's regional sales manager. Your request may not be well received by the supply representative, but their manager may see the value and agree. Whether the sales rep or a team member orders and restocks these supplies, a team member needs to be in charge of the outcome. Assign this role to the most likely person in the clinical operations column of your organizational chart, and be sure the integrator is copied on all orders.

Stocking

From your organization chart, determine the clinical team member who is in charge of clinical supplies. Ultimately, this person is in charge of restocking supplies, ensuring that back ordered items are put into the follow-up process, and making sure everything ordered was received. Hopefully, the dental supply representative is doing this for you, and they are accountable to run the system as designed. Even then, there will be occasions when this individual will not be able to unpack and restock product. Therefore, one team member should be in charge of making sure ordering and restocking is done on time and correctly, even if the supply representative is doing all the work.

Back-Ordered items

Use the same follow-up system that you have decided to use for the re-care scheduling or treatment coordinator's patient follow-up system. The office software system may provide a good follow-up system for you. If not, other software is available that can integrate with your office practice management software (e.g., Dental Intel). You can use a paper system, though it is more time-consuming. If you use a paper system, have an index-card-file box or a vertical paper-tray system with the twelve months of the year and weekly cards for each month. When a product is back-ordered, follow these steps:

- A shipping reconciliation sheet is placed into the weekly slot that corresponds with the date you expect the order to arrive.

- Circle back-ordered items so they are easily identified.

- When clinical supplies arrive, find the back-order sheet in the weekly organizer and cross off the back-ordered item(s).

- All back-ordered items may not arrive in the same shipment, so continue this step until all back-ordered items are crossed off.

- Throw away this sheet once all back-ordered items have been received.

Check this index-card file weekly. If a back-ordered product sheet is there for a week, check the central inventory area to see if it actually was received and was overlooked. If it hasn't been received, determine whether the item supply is dangerously low. If so, you may need to order from another source, or call your supply representative to get a new date when the back order will be shipped. Return the back-order paper into the tracking file under the new week that is consistent with when you expect the items to be received.

New Items

A new product may need to be ordered to replace an existing product, or you may decide to order a totally new item for clinical use.

For example, you purchase the office's first HuFriedy EMS system, and it has disposable supplies that will need to be ordered for the first time.

- The clinical manager submits a Clinical New Product Request Form to the in-charge person for clinical operations or the integrator, whichever is their immediate supervisor.

- This form is self-explanatory.

- The integrator or supervisor decides if the new product should be purchased.

- Decide how many units to start with.

- Decide when the item should be reordered.

- Decide how many units to reorder when reordering is necessary.

- Create a barcode or tag. Place the barcode or tag into the hygiene department products location in the central inventory area.

Our clinical operations manual is thorough and well over one hundred pages, so I am describing the tip of the iceberg. As you read the thoroughness of our system examples, do any of your systems need refinement? Perhaps you don't have a system manual, and now you see that by creating one, you'll save money and save your team time and frustration. Here is a list of other clinical systems to create greater office efficiency. Put a check mark next to all of these that you feel your office would benefit from, or add other processes or procedures currently used in your office that, once systematized, will produce improved consistency and quality.

- Chart notes

- Equipment repair

- Existing patients' images

- Light comm system

- Lab case flow

- Lab cleanliness

- Open/close office

- Pre-Tx Instructions

- Post-Tx Instructions

- Prescriptions

- OHI consistency

- CDA/doctor sales process

- Consents

- Sterilization

- Thank-you notes

- Video testimonials

- Asking for referrals

- Uniforms

- Operational cleanliness 🚩

KEY TAKEAWAYS

- Checklists are wonderful tools to keep the operatory organized so the dental assistant and dentist will spend the entire appointment helping the patient, not leaving the treatment room to get missing equipment or supplies. Patients notice your treatment flow. Lack of organization, someone leaving the room because you need something, or running out of any product in a procedure creates doubt in your ability to deliver the outcome patients expect. Additionally, a checklist allows the dental team to focus their thinking on the patient and the actual procedure rather than on interrupted thoughts on getting missing items.
- Creating a barcoded clinical supply system will provide proper supply overhead without excess stock, and flexibility to discontinue certain stocked items.
- Partner with the supply representative so your team can focus on more important tasks.

ACTION STEPS

- Identify one procedure when your assistant will sometimes leave the treatment room to get something that you knew you would need for that procedure. Have the assistant make a checklist to use while setting up the room for that procedure.
- Print a new checklist for each procedure on your schedule, and insist that every item on the checklist has a written check mark, indicating they put that item in the room. When the procedure goes smoothly, compliment your assistant. If they leave the room, use this opportunity to review how the checklist is to be used so that each item is placed in the

room, and then—and only then—is the check mark placed. Correct the bad habit of someone saying to themselves, "I'm going to get that item now, so I will check it off now to save me the time of checking it off when I actually get it." This is a good teaching moment for the assistant to understand the importance of a checklist, hold themselves accountable to an outcome, and further their individual growth into leadership.

- Call your dental supply representative and agree to use them as your sole source for small equipment, dental supplies, and equipment repair in exchange for them setting up and managing a barcoded product system.

- Additionally, have the supply representative come weekly to your office to open the product shipments, restock the shelves, and manage back orders and new orders. This system allows your dental supply representative to partner with you in exchange for you being their loyal customer.

PART IV

BUILDING WEALTH

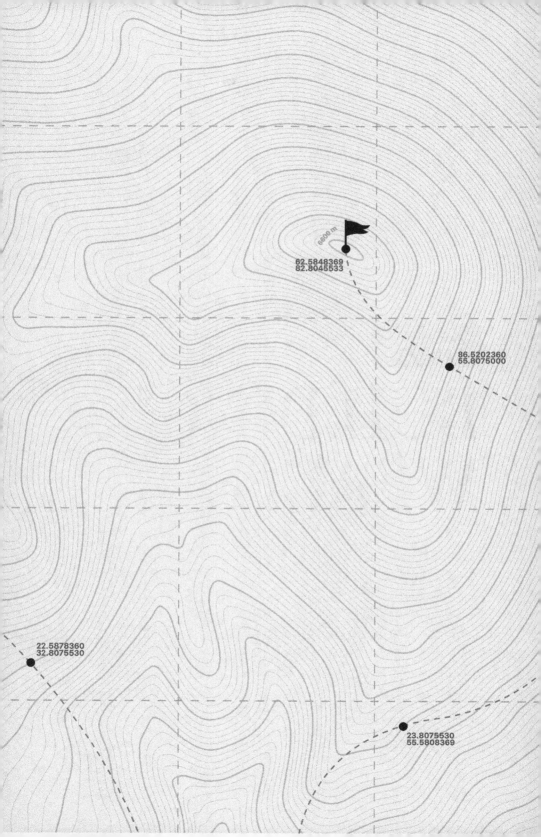

CHAPTER 8

Strategic Financial Planning

You don't have to be great to start, but
you have to start to be great.

—ZIG ZIGLAR

Earning money and having money may sound like two slices of the same pie, yet you must understand and respect the phrase "broke at different levels." What does that mean?

In 2009 the Trump Entertainment Resorts filed a Chapter 11,[9] which is a business bankruptcy filing. I recall reading a brief news article that interviewed Donald Trump and inquired how his lifestyle was doing now that his cash flow had been severely reduced. He commented that he had cut back immensely and that he was down to the lowest level that he could possibly live at, which was the $250,000 monthly expense total to keep his New York City penthouse apartment. In his mind, he was broke, with a severely restricted housing allowance of $3 million per year.

If you are willing to do the research, you will find countless individuals, like Mr. Trump in 2009, who are "broke," as defined by filing for bankruptcy or having properties repossessed due to lack of personal funds. Yet closer inspection will show that these people had vastly different income levels over their careers, with many earning significant six- and seven-figure incomes.

Statistically speaking, in 2021, the "average dentist" earned $180,000 per year, worked for forty-four years, and retired at age 68.8, while the average American earned one-third the amount of an average dentist and retired at age 62. So the higher-earning dentist retired five years later than the average American. Here are several factors that contribute to those statistics:

- Dentists are not business savvy and do not realize the importance of focusing on their wealth business just as much as their clinical business.

- Dentists are poor at delayed gratification. They graduate four to six years older than their counterparts. When they see their counterparts owning luxury items, they immediately

---

9   Peg Brickley, "Trump Entertainment Files Chapter 11 Turnaround Plan," wsj.com, October 1, 2014, https://www.wsj.com/articles/trump-entertainment-files-chapter-11-turnaround-plan-1412195699.

feel compelled to buy similar items. However, their counterparts have had four to six years of income and career growth/advancements to help pay for the luxury items with only four years of college debt, while the dentist has little initial income and eight to ten years of education debt.

- Dentists get used to living a finer life prior to retirement, so they expect the same or more in retirement. What they don't count on is that they will spend more money in retirement than they did while working simply because they have more available time to enjoy the purchase of tangible items or experiences such as trips and new adventures.

The financial end result of you being a better leader and your office running on better systems is that you will make more money. However, that alone doesn't guarantee you financial independence or a wonderful life after dentistry. This chapter will explore how you may look at your wealth from a mindset perspective and from a tactical perspective.

Decades ago, I recall being at a seminar presented by Greg Stanley, who reminded his dentist audience that "you are all just dentists—you're not rock stars, superathletes, Hollywood movie stars, or CEOs of Fortune 100 companies—you're just dentists." I smile when I recall those words since his message was that you and I need to be very intentional about what we do with every dollar we earn if we expect to "retire" in complete financial independence and have sufficient wealth to live well and thoroughly enjoy our retirement life.

Wealth Mindset

Evidence indicates that the crucial traits required to accumulate money or excel in other endeavors are evident by the age of four. A famous psychological study conducted in 1972 by Walter Mischel shed light on such essential characteristics and their behavioral choices.[10] Preschool children were given one marshmallow and told they would receive a second if they waited to eat the first marshmallow until the adult returned. Researchers filmed the children's conduct during these few minutes alone with the treats. Many ate the marshmallow, often within moments of the adult leaving. Those who waited and thus doubled their return visibly suffered, putting their hands over their eyes, singing, or walking around in courageous efforts to delay the pleasure of eating the

I will do today what others will not do so that I will have something tomorrow that others will not have.

marshmallow. Researchers followed these children throughout their school years. The ones who earned the second marshmallow significantly outperformed those who ate theirs in regard to their grades, test results, and virtually every factor measured. These children displayed delayed gratification ("I will do today what others will not do so that I will have something tomorrow that others will not have").

If you see yourself as the child who ate the marshmallow as soon as the researcher left the room, you aren't doomed to poverty. Yet you

---

10   Walter Mischel, The Marshmallow Test: Mastering Self-Control (New York, NY: Little, Brown Spark, 2014).

should look carefully at yourself and your mate when it comes to being resistant to putting money aside for future use. Take a moment to evaluate your personal history. How have you fared in your struggle to deny short-term pleasures and secure long-term investment gains? If your life history shows you tend to choose immediate gratification, but you're inspired to change, here's what you can do.

- **Increase your awareness.** The first essential ingredient is recognizing your behavior pattern and realizing options exist. Without this basic understanding, chances for meaningful change are slight.

- **Make a determined effort.** Being aware and wanting to change motivates you to make the necessary effort to obtain your desires. Set clear goals, such as saving the money needed before purchasing a car or notable office equipment rather than using debt.

In the bestselling book *The Millionaire Next Door: The Surprising Secrets of America's Wealthy*, Thomas J. Stanley and William D. Danko analyzed affluent individuals. They found that there are two types of millionaires: (1) those who inherit their wealth, and (2) those who are self-made millionaires. However, both types have the same intentional habit of spending less money than they make and saving the difference.

The Typical Millionaire

Eighty percent of millionaires are self-made, receiving no family money en route to becoming millionaires. They are typically forty-six years old, married with two or three children, and have an average annual income of $300,000, and their median net worth is $2.8

million. They work forty-five to fifty-five hours per week and tend to make investment decisions on their own or with some outside financial advisory.

Stanley and Danko repeatedly stress that the majority of self-made millionaires enjoy lifestyles of hard work, perseverance, planning, and self-discipline. How do their behaviors illustrate these values? Millionaires live well below their means. Most save 15 to 20 percent of their income and dedicate each month's first check to investments with the mantra, "Money never seen is money never missed." They understand that the opposite of frugal is wasteful and also understand that they can't spend themselves happy. Their partners are often planners and budgeters as well, and affluent husband-and-wife teams work together toward a well-defined mutual goal of wealth accumulation.

Cash Cow

While getting a positive return on your financial investment is important throughout most of your life, nothing will return you more dollars per hour than dentistry. I recommend you don't waste time and money on second businesses (as many bored dentists tend to do) or on investigating speculative exotics such as puts, calls, or commodity futures. Keep first things first and focus on continually becoming a better version of yourself and providing more and better optimal care for your patients. Dentistry is your cash cow and can create a fine income, so use this awesome financial vehicle to create the cash you need for your future (savings) as well as your current lifestyle.

Pay Yourself First

A common gambling phrase, "Take money off the table," describes what you should do when you are ahead of the house and you have made money at the card table. When you have made money in the card game, that is the time to take the amount of money you started with and put it into your pocket, where it is protected from you gambling it away.

Self-discipline is essential to attaining financial independence. You have self-discipline, or you wouldn't have made it through the rigors of a dental education. Unfortunately, once graduated and now making money, many dentists become compulsive spenders, purchasing not because of need or reason but because it feels good. Such wanton behavior creates unpredictable saving patterns so that what is saved is "whatever is left over." This approach is delusional at best because there's seldom anything remaining, resulting in little, if any, savings. This can be overcome by implementing a systematic investing approach by writing a check to your savings, no matter how small the amount, at the beginning of every month. This develops the habit of consistently saving and living on what is left.

When you are saving regularly, your money will be going to work for you, growing as it compounds and growing as you add more to it. If you forgo saving and your buying habits create debt, you become enslaved to the monthly debt payments. Money will work against you when paying debt and interest, or it will work for you and on your behalf when it is allowed to be saved and grow.

The intentional choice between saving (inflow) and spending (outgo) will determine whether you spend a joyous financial life flowing with abundant finances or an exhausting and stressful life paddling upstream against the strong current of debt.

The designation of this first monthly check has the power to determine one's future. It's that simple!

Automatic Withdrawals

There are many ways to put aside money so that you don't have the opportunity to spend it. You may feel you need lots of discipline to save money, and in reality, you only need a little discipline in the beginning. Set up automatic deposits so you don't rely on yourself to write a check every single week or month to put into a savings account. The discipline you need is simply to accept what I am saying as the absolute truth. Once you do that, set up the automatic removal of money from your practice and deposit it into an investment account. Once the automatic withdrawal vehicles are in place, you don't have to think about them, so no more discipline is required. The money simply flows out of your office into your accounts and immediately goes to work for you. Take advantage of dollar-cost averaging by making weekly deposits. Dollar-cost averaging simply means you are buying the same dollar amount of investment each week, not making any attempt to time your purchases. Over time, this strategy will prove to provide the greatest return on your invested money, and it eliminates the feeling of regret that occurs when you intentionally save money and then buy a stock, expecting it to go up, but it goes down. Weekly same-dollar-amount investing lets you buy more shares of stocks when their price is low and have fewer dollars exposed when their price is high. If you are new to investing, an investment account can be easily set up through one of the many investment companies such as Fidelity, Schwab, and Vanguard.

Increase Office Revenue and Profit

Right now, I will share with you the fastest and most predictable method to double or triple your office revenue and quadruple your profit: invest in yourself and your team. That is all you need to do, and you will see money flow into your life like never before.

Invest in People

Making yourself a better version of you will allow the greatest return of money possible. This book focuses on the business side of your practice, and making you the best version of you will provide joy, well-being, and peace.

I made myself a better clinical dentist version of myself by learning about and providing dental implants, bone grafting, clear aligners, IV sedation, and dental sleep medicine. Adding these services over four years resulted in my office revenue doubling to over $2 million and quadrupled profit. Everything being equal, the higher your revenue, the lower your overhead expense percentage becomes, providing more profit.

Investing in your team provides the second-greatest leverage to increasing revenue and business growth. Earlier chapters have discussed in detail the leadership responsibility you have to write down your business's noble purpose, create and review you and your team's core values, develop systems, and create an organizational chart so that each team member knows what they are responsible for. Also, have regular business meetings and learning meetings that provide team members with continual feedback on their success and continual personal and professional growth. I refer to the above as the team culture. An engaged team will create engaged patients who say yes to your optimal treatment, which creates increased revenue. When you commit to making your team the best they can be, they will want to propel your business to stratospheric levels.

Thus far in this chapter, I have shown you that unless you adopt the mindset that you must save regularly, you will never be wealthy since anyone can outspend their income. Additionally, I instructed you to invest in yourself and your team to propel your business into the cash cow it should be, spinning off profit that goes from your office into an investment account so that you never touch the money. Lastly, I want to briefly discuss how to increase your savable income through proper tax-reduction strategies and how to make investment decisions. All information that I present here is meant simply as a guide to get you thinking about different investment possibilities. This information is not meant to be instructional, so you need to speak with your financial advisors before making any pension, investment, or financial decisions. Ask your financial advisor what strategies are best for you right now, and continue to get their advice as your office revenue increases.

Investment Strategies

Investing your money simply means you are putting your money into a financial vehicle with the intention that it will grow in value over time. What vehicle you choose will be determined by your financial goals and your risk tolerance. I will walk you through the process of determining what your financial goals are. Risk tolerance is simply how comfortable you are with the possibility that the value of your money will go down or go to zero. For me, I invested as aggressively as I could to a point at which I was still able to sleep at night without worrying about changes in our investment portfolio.

Government-backed securities and FDIC-protected bank investments are the most conservative and safest since our federal institutions would have to default or collapse for you to lose your money. Government-backed and FDIC-protected investments include savings accounts and securities:

- Bank investments

    ▸ Savings accounts

    ▸ Money market funds

    ▸ Certificates of deposit (CDs)

- Government securities

    ▸ Treasury bonds

    ▸ Treasury bills

    ▸ Treasury notes

    ▸ Treasury inflation-protected securities (TIPS)

Other investment types are not backed by our government and therefore have greater risks:

- Annuities

- Commodities

- Cryptocurrency

- Derivatives

- Mutual funds / index funds / ETFs

- Real Estate

- Stocks/equities, including qualified retirement plans (QRPs)

- Tangible assets—precious metals

- Private equity

I cover these entities in depth in my individual coaching, and this book doesn't allow sufficient space to discuss them in detail. You may want to keep some money in government-backed investments so that you have immediate access to those funds, and they will not disappear when you need cash for predictable expenses. The larger your portfolio becomes, the more diversified you may decide to make it, and you may include more non-government-backed investments.

All information that I present here is meant simply as a guide to get you thinking of different investment possibilities. This information is not meant to be instructional, so you need to speak with your financial advisors before making any pension, investment, or financial decisions. Ask your financial advisor what strategies are best for you right now, and continue to get their advice as your office revenue increases. Here are some tax-saving strategies you can explore with your financial advisors to see if they fit with your goals and objectives.

- Family members on office payroll

- 529 educational plan

- Health savings account (HSA)

- Home-based management business

- Insurance products

- Office and personal expense overlap

Like the investment strategies, I cover these entities in depth in my individual coaching, and this book doesn't allow sufficient space to discuss them in detail. I encourage you to sit with your financial advisors and consider implementing these strategies. Once they are in place, they go to work reducing your tax bill and increasing your available investment dollars.

Retirement Goals

If you are nearing "retirement age," then retirement is often on your mind, while if you are young, retirement is rarely on your mind. Either way, I want to help you create a viable retirement blueprint.

First, dispel the myth that you will spend less in retirement. You will have more available free time, and many retired dentists spend 20 to 40 percent more than they spent when seeing patients four days a week. More free time equates to more travel expenses and more time to enjoy newly purchased items.

Second, don't include Social Security payments in your calculations. Our government is severely overleveraged, and you do not want to count on those payments. Consider them as ice cream on the cake, not an ingredient in the cake.

> **Once you get closer to retirement, you'll know better if you are motivated to create an income stream outside of your investment portfolio's passive income.**

Third, don't count on creating a source of income outside your dental practice once you sell it. You may create another company and therefore create another earned income stream, yet do not think that will be for sure. Once you get closer to retirement, you'll know better if you are motivated to create an income stream outside of your investment portfolio's passive income.

Fourth, you must decide whether you will gradually spend all of your retirement portfolio and risk running out of money before you run out of life or allow the principal derived from your investment portfolio to grow indefinitely while you live off the dividends, interest, or rent payments spun off from your portfolio. Again, talk with your financial advisor, who can help guide you through these questions.

Knowing these four conditions, here is an example of how you can decide how much money you have to have to retire financially free. You can substitute your numbers while keeping the formulas the same.

- **Step 1.** OK, I'm "just a dentist," so I am focused on making myself and my dental office more profitable every year.

- **Step 2.** My annual expenses are $180,000, so I need at least $90,000 in my personal checking account to have the recommended six months' cash reserve. The checking account has had over $110,000 for the last several months, so I transfer $30,000 to my personal brokerage investment account, putting it to work rather than sitting in my bank account, earning savings account returns.

- **Step 3.** My office revenue is $1.2 million per year, and the overhead before I pay myself is $780,000, so the remaining "profit" is $420,000. Of the $780,000, $46,000 is going into my qualified retirement plan (QRP) accounts. I need to invest 25 percent of the profit, so $420,000 x .25 = $105,000. $105,000-$46,000 (QRPs in my name) = $59,000. I need to invest $59,000 more.

- **Step 4.** Because $59,000/52 weeks per year = $1,135 per week, I need to move money from my office checking account to my investment account via an ACH transfer. With the advice from my financial advisors, I instructed the investment firm how I want my investment portfolio allocated to meet my growth objectives and goals. I touch base with my financial advisors at least annually to reevaluate those objectives; otherwise it is a simple plug-and-play.

- **Step 5.** Our current living expenses, including federal and state income tax, are $180,000. I want to retire in eighteen years. I currently have $750,000 in my QRP accounts and $70,000 in my personal brokerage investing account. Therefore, my total current investments equal $820,000. In retirement, I'll spend at least 25 percent more than now, so 180,000 + (180,000 x 25 percent) = $225,000. I use the compounding-interest calculator at www.thecalculatorsite.com to determine how much money to save every month for the next eighteen years, so that eighteen years from now, I will have a big enough portfolio (my money tree) so that the fruit that falls off the money tree (dividends, interest—money I can spend) will equal $225,000 per year. I will assume the portfolio will have an average growth of 5 percent per year.

    The math: 5 percent of $X (total portfolio at retirement) = $225,000. X = $4.5 million. So I need $4.5 million at retirement, which will provide me $225,000 of spendable income per year. I currently have $820,000, so for the next eighteen years, how much must I invest each month, at a 5-percent-per-year return on investment, so that eighteen years from now I will have $4.5 million?

    Go to: https://www.thecalculatorsite.com/finance/calculators/compoundinterestcalculator.php and plug in the values. You'll find that the monthly investment you have to make is $7,300 for the next eighteen years, at a 5 percent return to have $4.5 million at retirement: $7,300 x 12 = $87,600/year, and $87,600/52 weeks per year = $1,685. Each week you deposit $1,865 to your personal brokerage account via ACH transfer. Therefore, based on your current office revenue, you need to save more than 25 percent to reach your goal. There are many variables, but you get the idea. If you will be funding the office QRPs during those eighteen years, then subtract the prior year's personal QRP deposit from $87,600 to determine the weekly ACH transfer. Suppose you have not been funding your QRPs or you want to retire sooner than eighteen years from now. Let's quickly explore those scenarios.

Instead of $750,000 in your QRP accounts, you have $350,000. Doing all the same math with this one changed variable, you would need to invest $2,330 per week. That equals $645 more per week, or $34,000 more per year. If you said you wanted to retire in ten years, not eighteen, you would need to invest $5,538 per week to reach your $4.5 million goal. Yikes! You can appreciate the power, or liability, of compounding and how reducing the amount of time the money can compound and grow severely affects the total value of the investments.

Now that you know your number, I will offer you guidance on when to invest and what investment vehicles to use at each stage of your business growth. Understand that you need a certain amount of office revenue to afford different types of investment strategies. As always, you'll want to sit down with your financial advisors. You may decide to share this information with them so they can best help you decide what fits with your current finances and your short-term and long-term financial goals.

When and How to Invest

Revenue: Less Than $500,000 per Year

With office revenue less than $500,00, consider fully funding your IRA and aggressively putting the rest of the office "profit" back into you, your team, and the office, as described above. At this low revenue, you are likely a young dentist, so you have many years of clinical dentistry ahead of you before you retire. That said, if you and your spouse or significant other invested the annual maximum IRA ($6,500 per person in 2022) each year, from age twenty-seven until retirement at age sixty-two, you would have $3.9 million at retirement, $3 million of which would be interest. Amazing, right?

Revenue: $750,000 to $1 Million

As you push your office revenue toward the $1 million mark, consider continuously investing in your IRA, and consider adding a 401(k) plan to your office. The 401(k) allows your employees to start saving some of their own money, and you, the employer, are not required to add money to the employee's accounts. To fully maximize the total dollars invested into this type of plan, you may want to add a safe harbor and profit-sharing component. For me, I expected to receive 88 percent of all 401(k) contributions. The employees received the remaining 12 percent that the business put into our plan. This type of plan legally needs to have a third-party administrator to handle the funding and the reporting to the IRS. Either they or your financial advisors will calculate different funding scenarios, and they will help you decide what level of funding is best for you. Since this vehicle allows the business to put money into the employees' retirement plan, you'll need to decide how "generous" you want to be. If your salary package is average, perhaps this benefit is appreciated by your employees.

One warning: Not to sound cynical, but your employees will likely take all pension benefits for granted because they cannot spend it today, and many dental office employees live paycheck to paycheck. A 2022 survey showed that 63 percent of Americans live paycheck to paycheck. Even more interesting is that of the Americans whose household income is greater than $100,000 per year, a full 50 percent also live paycheck to paycheck. Therefore, the purpose of the 401(k) is for you, the doctor, to have a disciplined vehicle to save money for your retirement. The fact that your team gets some of the money is a very nice benefit to them, but that is not the objective.

> **Key concept:** The purpose of office QRPs is for you, the doctor, to put money away for retirement.

Assuming you and your spouse are both maximally funding your 2022 401(k) accounts, you can contribute $45,000 per year. If you started funding your 401(k) accounts at age thirty-eight and continued until age sixty-two, these accounts would grow to $6.6 million, of which $4.5 million would be interest-only growth. Consider that our example of using just the IRA and the 401(k) together had created a $10.5 million retirement fund. Pretty nice with just those two vehicles. As an aside, I suspect the US individual income tax rates will increase from where they are now. If your advisors feel the same way, you may consider putting some or all of these funds into a Roth 401(k). You'll pay the tax now so your retirement withdrawals will be tax-free. That certainly will be nice if the United States should ever get back to the 50 percent to 80 percent maximum income tax brackets we had as recently as 1980.

Revenue: $1 Million to $1.5 Million

You have been in practice for seven to ten years, and now you have surpassed the $1 million mark in office revenue (likely much sooner than seven to ten years if you have used our business coaching program). The growth from $800,000 to $1.3 million is a big number—$500,000—yet it happens very quickly for the offices that have implemented sound systems, are working on their Leader-Leader culture, and have invested in themselves and their teams. The party begins at this level of revenue and above. If you and your financial advisors agree, you may be able to fully fund your IRA and your 401(k) and still have money left over to invest elsewhere. How you invest from this point on depends on your investing philosophy, your risk tolerance, and your interest in exploring the many other investing vehicles. If you like the idea of counting on the stock market to give you historical 8-percent-per-year returns, then you may want to explore setting up a defined benefit plan. For me, I was much older than my team, so I received about 95 percent of the dollars that were deposited into the account when I sold the business.

CAPTIVE INSURANCE POLICY

A captive insurance policy may be worth your consideration at this point since you can fund it to whatever dollar amount you wish. You'll pay 10 to 12 percent of the premium toward administration costs; the leftover money is yours, and this does not involve your employees, so you are not making contributions on their behalf. There are essentially no limits as to how little or how much you contribute to a microcaptive. After expenses, the remaining funds are yours, they grow tax-free, and they are treated like ordinary income when you liquidate the captive at retirement.

NON-QRPS

Alternatively, you may have a higher tolerance for risk and want to consider making weekly contributions to a personal brokerage account or to your personal savings account. With these funds, you'll be able to invest in annuities, REITS, and some of the other investments we discussed and have the freedom to liquidate the investment and use it for other non-QRP investments. For instance, you can use QRP funds to invest in real estate, as long as you don't want to ever live in the property or rent it to yourself. Doing so is against QRP rules, and you'll pay hefty penalties when you are caught. However, you can sweep money out of your office into your personal bank account, purchase investment property in a warm, sunny place, and use it some and rent it out some. You get the investment advantages, and you can use and enjoy the property as you wish.

Revenue: $1.5 Million to $3 Million

As you push your office revenue past $2 million into the mid-$2.5-million area, your office profit is climbing into the seven-figure stratosphere. This is an excellent time to be sure you are looking at your current lifestyle, what your retirement lifestyle will look like, and most importantly, what your retirement number needs to be. At this annual "income" level, the difference between the men and the boys is the price of their toys. Items that you never thought you would own or want start to become possible. Large boats and yachts, multiple homes, airplanes/jets, high-end cars, and other expensive hobbies all become possible. This is perhaps the most dangerous financial time in your life. Money will be pouring into your life from everywhere, and you'll likely have met some other entrepreneurs who are introducing you to their toys. Keep in mind that your friend's manufacturing business may only spin off $1 million per year for the owner, but the stock options and other financial benefits that they enjoy may push their net worth to $100 million. His ability to "afford" certain toys may outstrip yours. Keep your focus on your own goals, and don't get seduced into making purchases where the upkeep alone creates a strain on your current or retirement budget.

You may want to chat with your financial advisors about diversifying your portfolio of investments to include angel investing or venture capital

Keep your focus on your own goals, and don't get seduced into making purchases where the upkeep alone creates a strain on your current or retirement budget.

investing. These investments are speculative, yet when they are well thought-out and well played, they can offer a handsome ROI. The goal of venture capital is to get returns on investment in the 3x to 5x range, with the outside hope of an incredible winner creating a 20x to 100x return. Of course, you can lose all your investment as well—high reward means high risk. We encourage you to be very cautious in this arena, but being cautious doesn't mean to stay away. You can consider allocating some of your investing funds to dip your toe into this area. Typically, you'll need to allow two to seven years to see any return on your capital investment, so these are not liquid plays, but they can create a very handsome windfall. All information that I present here is meant simply as a guide to get you thinking of different investment possibilities. This information is not meant to be instructional, so you need to speak with your financial advisors before making any pension, investment, or financial decisions. Ask your financial advisor what strategies are best for you right now, and continue to get their advice as your office revenue increases.

Beyond these guidelines of when to move money and into which vehicles, there are many conversations about portfolio diversification. A common rule of thumb is to have 60 to 70 percent in stocks, 20 to 30 percent in bonds, and 5 to 10 percent in real estate. The younger you are, and therefore the more years until "retirement," the more aggressive you may decide to be. Bonds are meant to conserve your portfolio, so they are a defensive play, looking to avoid losses as opposed to creating gains. You'll have to decide if you want to self-direct none, some, or all of your investments based on your personal interest (and acumen) as an investor. If you try paper trading and find you don't like it or you don't keep up with it, please don't kid yourself by self-directing all your actual money investments. You will be wasting your precious time doing something you're not good at, and you'll be wasting the compounding time for good investments to grow. A general dentist can take many CE courses and master the same standard of care as a specialist. You can do the same with investing if you become a student of investing. On the other hand, if you see the value of referring dental procedures to specialists, then do the same with your money when it is out of your wheelhouse.

Identify where you are in your journey to financial freedom. Are you ahead of schedule, or perhaps behind where you should be? Either way, you just empowered yourself by knowing the answer to this question. With that knowledge, what will be the first step you can take to advance your money tree? Take the time to identify one change in how you think about wealth, what the first move you make will be to have the greatest impact on your future wealth, and the speed you arrive at financial freedom. Always be ready to speak with your financial advisors before making any pension, investment, or financial decisions. Their advice is extremely valuable, and I encourage you to have regular conversations with each individual on your financial advisory team. ⚑

KEY TAKEAWAYS

- Dentists are historically poor at delayed gratification, which results in their working four years longer than the average American. We dentists earn more than the average American, which often results in the false belief that we don't need to save now because we will make even more money as our practice grows. The power of compounding growth works exceedingly well over a longer time frame, so begin regular investing at a young age.
- Until you have several million dollars in your investment portfolio, your office will be your best investment for the highest return on money invested. Attend courses that teach you and your team to be better leaders and clinical courses that foster the addition of more lucrative procedures to your current service mix with the goal of increasing hourly revenue. Continue viewing your office as the primary source of income (your cash cow) so that 5 percent of your investment portfolio is the same dollar amount as your office's annual profit. The goal is for 5 percent of your investment

portfolios to be equal to or greater than your earned income from dentistry.

ACTION STEPS

- Identify one clinical procedure you could add to your current mix if you were to go to a continuing education course. Determine how much the course and subsequent equipment or supplies will cost and what fee you will charge patients for that procedure.
- Then do the math to determine how many of these procedures you'll need to do to get all your initial investment back. I suspect you will find several procedures that fit with your current service mix and will provide a 100 percent return in less than six months.
- Calculate your current living expenses, then use my formulas to determine the amount of money you will need in your retirement portfolio in order to retire financially free with an enhanced retirement lifestyle.

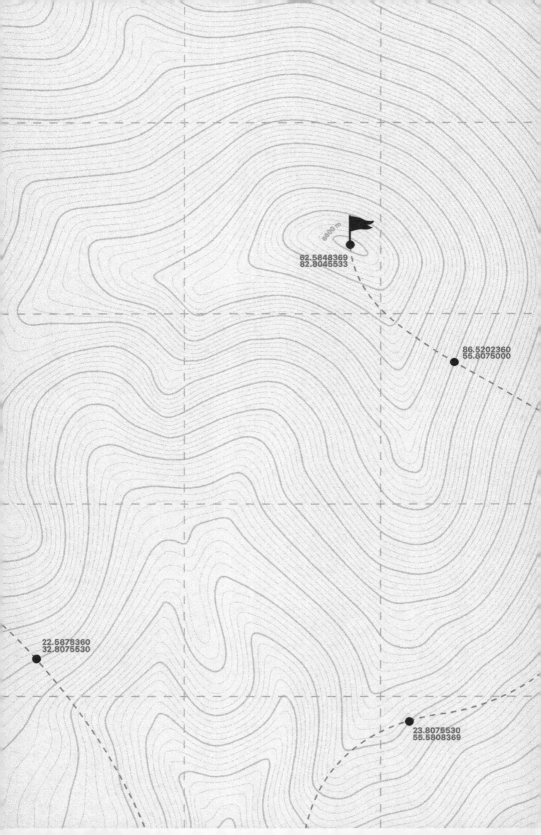

6600 m

62.5848369
82.8045533

86.5202360
55.8075000

22.5878360
32.8075530

23.8075530
55.5808369

CHAPTER 9

Wealth Accumulation and Legacy Development

Nothing is more difficult, and therefore more precious, than to be able to decide.

—NAPOLÉON BONAPARTE

How and when to retire are the two decisions that seem easy to some dentists and cause much worry for other dentists. That said, it is difficult to know whether the relaxed dentist or the troubled dentist will end up feeling fulfilled in retirement. This last chapter of my book is designed to help you be sure you design the retirement chapter of your life to be a huge success.

I met Jim at a dental conference where each dentist was discussing the successes and challenges they have in their dental practices. Jim was very passionate when he described how much he liked dentistry yet how much he disliked his team. "All they do is bitch and complain about everything, and I dread going to work." Jim had enough gray hair that I asked if he had any retirement plans. He said he would love to retire, but he didn't know if he could. A few questions and answers later, I knew Jim wasn't confident in how much money he would need to retire, and if he knew that number and could get that amount of money, he would retire immediately. I emailed Jim the math puzzle I just shared with you and told him to fill it out and run the numbers by his financial advisors. I said Jim should then hire a dental broker just to evaluate his practice's sale value so he would know what similar practices had recently sold for within one hundred miles of his practice. I saw Jim at another conference three months later, where he held out his hand and said, "Thank you so much for the information you sent me. I hired a broker the next day, did the math problem you sent me, and ran the numbers by my advisors. As of two weeks ago, I have an LOI to sell my practice." He was ecstatic! He learned that he needed to add $800,000 to his "money tree" in order to retire, and the broker suggested his practice would sell for $750,000 to $925,000. With the money from the projected sale of his dental office, Jim's money tree would now have enough so he could live in retirement on the dividends from his investment portfolio.

For Jim, this was new thinking and an "aha" moment, helping him make a confident decision. I had been making those same calculations for decades for myself. At age thirty-five, I knew what I wanted to be financially free at age fifty. At age fifty-three, I was financially free. However, I enjoyed the dental profession, so I decided to keep working. My practice kept growing, we had more revenue, and I started developing some expensive recreational tastes. I found that high-altitude backpack hunting for sheep and goats in some of the most remote areas of the world requires a different retirement "money tree" than the one I was cultivating at age thirty-five. My wife wanted to realize her lifelong dream to live in a custom-built contemporary oceanfront beach house. That required a different "money tree" than the one I was cultivating at age fifty. From age fifty-three to sixty-two, we continued to add to our money tree while routinely recalculating the math to make sure we were on target. Now that we are enjoying our Florida beach house and our Montana mountain home, my wife describes the two of us as "kids with money."

My friend Steve has worked for years as an executive coach and has had countless conversations with entrepreneurs who sell their businesses and go into retirement for the wrong reasons or at the wrong time. He "warned me" that when I sold my practice, my perception of myself and the world's perception of me would change. His concerns are well founded since for all of us, some of our ego is wrapped around being called "Doctor" and being in charge of the office, and perhaps with having our name on the sign. When you sell your business, all that comes to a screeching halt. You can keep your dental license and introduce yourself as Dr. _____, and then you'll be forced to answer questions about what kind of doctor you are and where you practice. The world seems to stop respecting the degree when you are no longer practicing, and your ego must be ready for that.

Many of you have nondentist friends who retire, and a little while into retirement, they go back to work at the same company, or they get a completely different job. These individuals were not prepared for retirement, and that explains the gap between retiring and going back to work. Retirement was not what they thought it would be, so they went to work again.

Transitions

There are several different ways to transition from full-time work as a dentist/owner to complete retirement, and I will make a case for each to help you decide what fits best with your life. Your decision will revolve around the following factors:

- Do you need additional money to complete your "money tree"?

- Do you still love clinical dentistry and going to work?

- Do you like running the business side of your practice?

- When you're fully retired, what purpose will get you out of bed?

- Do you practice alone, or with partners, or do associate dentists work for you?

Transition A. If you still need money to complete your money tree, my strong advice is to keep practicing, unless your advisors are certain the sale of your office will complete your investment portfolio and allow for your financial freedom. Retirement can be disheartening when your retirement lifestyle is below your working lifestyle because you don't have enough money to live at the same level. If the practice sale will complete your money tree, then determine how bruised your ego will be without a place where you are king or queen? If your ego will be OK, then have you determined what your life purpose will be in retirement? Individuals end up going back to work after a short retirement due to boredom and feeling marginalized by society.

Transition B. If you still love clinical dentistry and you are approaching retirement age, then the questions change a little. First, if your money tree isn't full, follow the advice in Transition A. If your money tree is full, then you may want to consider practicing dentistry as a hobby—you don't need the money to be financially free; you are doing it strictly for pleasure. I am not suggesting you don't like the money, since I already told you that I love money because it is an amazing tool for many creative outcomes.

The next question is: Do you enjoy the business side of dental office ownership? A neighbor and friend of mine, Greg, practiced dentistry for thirty years before deciding he didn't like the business side of dentistry and loved the clinical side. The best advice for him was to find a successful entrepreneurial dentist who was willing to purchase his business outright or partner with Greg. I recommend that you keep at least 51 percent ownership since I have seen several dentists that sold with the "understanding" that they would stay on as an employee for as long as they wanted. Within a few years, they were forced to leave with no legal recourse but to do so. If you want to stay on and will take in a partner, be sure the partner has very good business skills and is prepared to accept full responsibility for that role. I highly recommend *The Partnership Charter*, by David Gage, for any dentist who will be hiring an associate who wants eventual ownership. I recommend the same read before you entertain any partnership arrangement. Gage's book will force each side to consider virtually all potential pitfalls and address them so you have an agreement on what you will do before each situation arises. An ounce of prevention is worth a pound of cure.

Transition C. You love all aspects of being a dentist/owner, your money tree is complete, and you work by yourself. Your questions surround how you want to sell your practice when the time comes. Do you want to leave a legacy and see the practice continue serving the community with optimal dentistry? Additionally, do you practice in a very desirable geographic area that dentists will easily move to? A good friend of mine and a senior dentist, Bill, lives in a rural area of New York State and has an enviable practice with great numbers, a modern facility, and a strong team. He wants to reduce his hours and then sell. I can sympathize with his predicament, which is that he cannot attract an excellent dentist to his rural geographic location. Bill's journey is similar to mine in that he started out as an average dentist who was on a mission. Over time, he developed his amazing skill set and lifestyle in this small north-country town. Young dentists, who might love to work in his practice, may not want to move to the small rural town. An older dentist who may have the money to buy the practice may not have the skill set to create the practice's revenue. Bill's future may well be like mine, which is to sell the practice for a fraction of the calculated value because an attractive and qualified buyer cannot be found. If you live in a geographic area that doesn't attract younger dentists, then I suggest you start looking many years before you intend to retire. Eventually, you will likely find a good buyer, though you will need to be more patient and persistent than the dentist who practices in a very desirable location to live in, meet a life partner, and raise a family.

Transition D. You love the business side of dentistry, and you do not want to continue practicing clinical dentistry. If your money tree is full, then you have several options, though I feel they are not equal. A primary question is: Do you enjoy living in the town where you are now or where you live now? In my case, I was excited to move out of New York State for the rest of my life. I have a colleague who has not practiced in his dental office for twenty years and manages it from the other side of the country. However, this is not something that works for me. I have always felt one of my primary jobs as the leader is to remind the team who we are and what our behavior needs to be to uphold our noble purpose and core values. I am unsure of how successful I can be without ever stepping foot in the office and still maintaining an office culture that is delivering optimal full-mouth dentistry. If I owned an office that was doing routine restorative dentistry and not providing full-mouth dentistry, I feel I could manage this office at a distance as long as the office was in a geographically desirable location. Again, if the office is in an undesirable location, the loss of an associate dentist can severely handicap the practice revenue, and the owner might be forced to consider returning to practice clinical dentistry while an associate search takes place. Alternatively, the owner may need to consider selling to a corporate dental entity that can bring in an associate dentist to keep the practice viable.

When you have decided you are emotionally ready to leave your business and your money

> **When you have decided you are emotionally ready to leave your business and your money tree is full, spend time determining what your purpose will be once you hang up your loupes.**

tree is full, spend time determining what your purpose will be once you hang up your loupes. I am envious of any individual who can stop having a dentistry-earned income and fill the rest of their days with self-serving recreation and regular local volunteer efforts. This seems like such an easy and sustainable retirement life to me, but it simply doesn't fit my personality or mindset. I enjoy creating, learning, being adventurous, and making a significant difference in the world. I am an introvert, so it's draining to spend my day surrounded with people. In the four to five years before selling my office, I intentionally explored what I would do after the sale so I would not go into a retirement void. That is what I had to do and from that arose my coaching business, Ultimate Success in Dentistry.

Should you decide you will sell your practice, and you do not have an associate or partner to sell to, I will make the following recommendations:

- Use a broker, as they will give you the best exposure to multiple potential buyers at once, which can force a more competitive selling advantage.

- Broker fees and the length of exclusivity are negotiable. All brokers will tell you they have a list of potential clients, and they want an exclusive contract for twelve months and 8 to 10 percent commission. They may have a few potential clients, and once they show them your practice, they either buy it, or their list goes to zero. Then they are waiting for the phone to ring for another potential buyer, just like every other broker. They want twelve months of exclusivity just to get your practice off the market and on their books, not because they have some amazing ability to find potential buyers. Their commission can be negotiated down to 6 percent, and it can be tiered, with their percentage going up as the sale price goes up. This encourages them to sell it at the highest fee they can, and it holds them accountable to their assessed value of your practice. For instance, if the broker tells you they will sell your office for $1.5 million, and they offer you an 8 percent commission, but you suspect the office will sell closer to $1.2 million, you can suggest that they earn a 6 percent commission up to $1.2 million and then 8 percent on everything over $1.2 million. If you own your office building and you want to sell that as well, the broker has no reason to earn a commission on the sale of the building. Find another broker if they make that a contingency of their contract with you.

- Once you know you will be selling your practice, carefully go through your accounts receivable, and eliminate any balances where you owe patients less than $50 and the accounts are more than three years old. This action cannot be reckless, though. You might, for example, discover small account balances that have been owed to patients for many years, and you cannot locate them to send them the money. If you leave these accounts on your books, your agreed-upon sale price will be reduced dollar for dollar, since the new owner will justify that they will have to pay these funds to your patients. But in reality, they will keep the money because they will not be able to find the patients to get it to them either. I strongly recommend you discuss this process with your CPA and legal team, as you want to make sure you abide by the rules of your state, and you use proper ledger entries.

As you think about transitioning out of your business, determine if you are most concerned with

- not having your money tree full,

- not having a retirement life purpose,

- dealing with not being the king of your business any longer, or

- missing the clinical or business aspect of dentistry.

Start now to determine what you need to do so that your retirement days can be like my wife's and mine—happy and fulfilled kids with money! ⚑

KEY TAKEAWAY

- There are numerous methods to transition away from full-time dentistry into the next phase of your life. Your task is to look at yourself and see which transition style works best for you. Once you are clear on what you need for your transition to be successful, begin putting the pieces of the puzzle together to make it happen. Formulate a plan when you are early in your career, knowing that it may well change. You are much better off to have thought out a plan that never came to be than to have not thought out a plan and feel forced to take retirement actions you resent or regret.

ACTION STEP

- Write down each of the four transitions, and next to each, write the pros and the cons. Force yourself to go back to this document once a week for eight weeks. Be prepared to add items to the pros and cons for each item, and *never* subtract something that you wrote as a pro or a con. Your mood and life in general will affect what you write down, so allow yourself the freedom to continuously add your thoughts. After eight weeks, with eight different looks at your transition options, your current best choice will become clear. Once you know what you want the end of your transition to look like, you can reverse-engineer to create the action steps that must happen to stay on your chosen transition path.

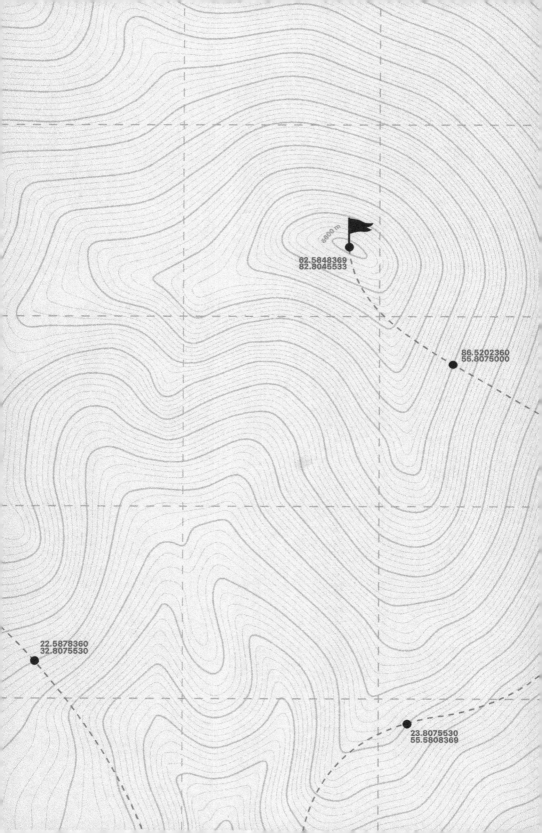

6800 m

62.5848369
82.8045533

86.5202360
55.8075000

22.5878360
32.8075530

23.8075530
55.5808369

Conclusion

Success in dentistry embodies the same attributes and process as success in any life endeavor. Fleeting success can occur with luck, while sustained success is entirely intentional. Enduring success requires showing up every day, prepared to give it your best. The process begins with being able to see where you are going. To feel the pain and to relish the victory. To hear the roar of the crowd, even if the crowd is only in your mind as you stand alone with your fists held high in victory. Seeing yourself as the leader you want to be is a great challenge. Perhaps that process starts with imagining the exact opposite of what is happening now. If your morning huddle seems unproductive, what does it look like to have a morning huddle that is productive and engaging? When you have had poor conversations with underperforming team members, picture what type of conversation you want to have next time. How does a leader respond to a team member whose actions consistently oppose the core values of your organization?

The mechanics of setting up operational systems to run your office and to create personal financial wealth are indeed necessary. I have met numerous individuals who have a wonderful view of the world or themselves, and they make wonderful contributions to the lives of individuals and society. Yet they failed to see the need to create systems in their own lives to achieve organization and financial freedom. If you are one of the fortunate people who has mastered the art of good thinking, seek out and empower others who can create, implement, and maintain these systems for you. These systems are necessary and mechanical, so someone can put that together for you.

Thinking well and creating a successful mindset is on you. Intentionally surround yourself with people who will challenge and uplift you. Become a fervent reader of success principles as they relate to your awareness around thinking, mindset, and success. When you meet the teacher who has the respect and command of your child, be curious about how they think, and learn from their mastery.

> **See the change you want in your mind, and then step into your life and make it happen.**

I have given you many examples of specific techniques to have conversations, organize processes, and create wealth. Put in place those that resonate with you and will improve your business and personal life. Whenever you aren't getting the results you desire, know that you have control over the outcome since you are the problem and you are the magic. See the change you want in your mind, and then step into your life and make it happen.

Can you visualize the Iditarod sled dog race with the dogsled, dogs, and musher? The musher alternates between standing on the sled and pushing from the rear, always aware when his team needs encouragement, challenge, direction, and rest. I love that visual when I look at leadership in the dental office. The team is excited about the race, though they know it is a journey, and my role as the commander and leader is to provide direction and the guiding hand. Some dentists I speak with, and those I coach, see themselves strapped into the front of the sled harness with some team members out of the harness, sitting on the sled, or simply standing around. These dentists feel they are the only one in their office actively pulling the sled, and they are full of unrelenting frustration and exhaustion.

At this phase in my life journey, my purpose is to help those dentists right their sleds and allow their teams to do the heavy lifting so that together, they can accomplish many individual wins and patient/team victories. Life is short. You deserve to have an amazing dental career with no regrets and the opportunity to enjoy the view from life's highest peaks.

I invite you to connect with me at www.UltimateSuccess.Dentist. There you'll find free templates and downloadable worksheets that may help you work through the exercises in this book. And if it makes sense, I am willing to discuss how else I may help you in your journey to having a fulfilled dental life with financial freedom and many peaks of success.

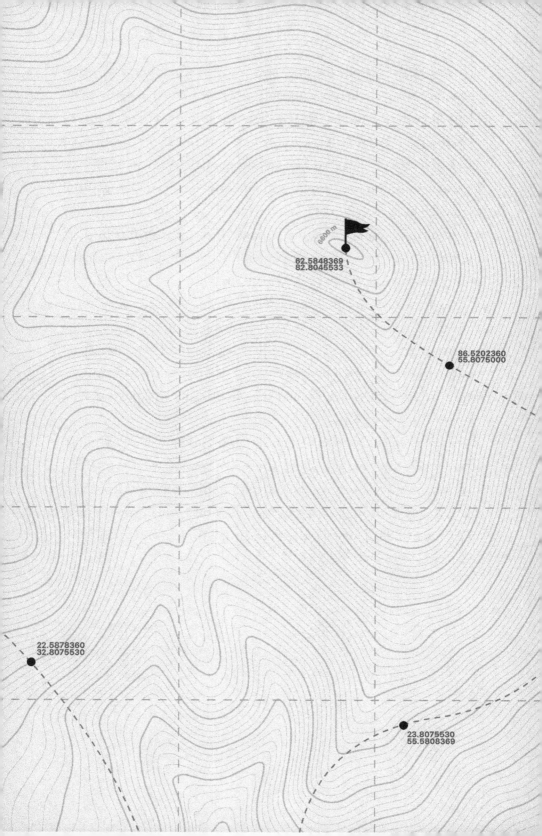

Acknowledgments

If you want to go fast, go alone. If you want to go far, go together.

—AFRICAN PROVERB

I have gleaned so much from many teachers and individuals that to pick out a few is difficult. That said, I want to single out four individuals who provided me with the insights, ideas, and infinite support to make this book come to fruition. I'd like to sincerely thank my mentor and friend, Master Scott Manning, for his unending ability to see me where I am, elevate the bar to who he knows I can be, and provide the guidance and resources for me to get there. I'd also like to thank Dr. Daniel Klauer, a truly amazing individual who continues to succeed in dentistry and life like no single dentist that I have ever met. Thank you for your ever-present support, your specific directional references, and your constant push to reset the bar ever higher. I also want to thank Dr. Andy Bartish for all his support and encouragement in creating content for interviews and his insightful business development concepts. Never last, I'd like to thank my son-in-law, Jim Murphy, for his constant support and book creation ideas that pique my initial authorship interests and continue to fuel my writing.

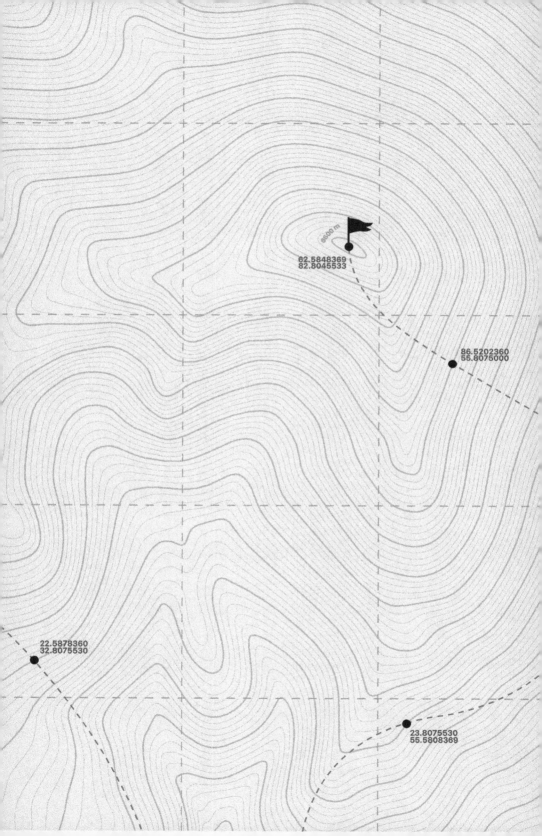

About the Author

David Richard Pearce is an example of what makes the United States of America the greatest nation in the world, because it is in this country that anyone can achieve what they want if they are willing to have the discipline and desire to do so. Dr. Pearce's parents encouraged him to get a job as a dentist with the State of New York, where he grew up, as that would provide him with the safe and predictable life they had created for themselves. While Dr. Pearce enjoyed his childhood friends, many of his fondest memories are when he was by himself in the woods, creating a make-believe world of challenge and victory, or in the home basement, constructing mechanical creations out of available toy parts or scrap wood.

Always a polite, quiet, humble, and confident young man, Dr. Pearce never saw himself as an employee because being told how to run his day or his life just didn't fit. In 1984, he bought his first practice in Keene, New Hampshire, and there he met three dentists who introduced him to the Pankey Institute and, more importantly, the idea of looking at the entire mouth rather than just fixing one tooth at a time. As a consummate student and lifelong learner, over his clinical career, Dr. Pearce spent over five thousand hours traveling and learning how to craft his skill while becoming a Kois Center mentor and a board-certified diplomate in dental sleep medicine, with fellowships in the ICOI and MIII, IV sedation certification, and much more. At the same time, Dr. Pearce's strong interest in business, money, and finance fueled his pursuit to learn methods to make his business profitable, extract money from his business, and invest that money to ensure an independently wealthy and financially free life. At age fifty-eight, Dr. Pearce and his wife, Susan, became financially independent. He practiced for another six years, continuing to refine his office systems to drive team member leadership skills and improve his relationship-based full-mouth reconstructive practice.

Today, Dr. Pearce has exited the clinical dentistry phase of his life journey and is helping other dentists achieve the results he did, but much faster, through his individual coaching and leadership summits at Ultimate Success in Dentistry. Having walked the walk, Dr. Pearce has the passion and ability to guide any dentist who wants to provide optimal full-mouth care while simultaneously creating a financially free and independent lifestyle. ⚑

Printed in the USA
CPSIA information can be obtained
at www.ICGtesting.com
JSHW082204140824
68134JS00014B/413